FOOD CHAINS AND ECOSYSTEMS

FOOD CHAINS AND ECOSYSTEMS

Ecology for Young Experimenters

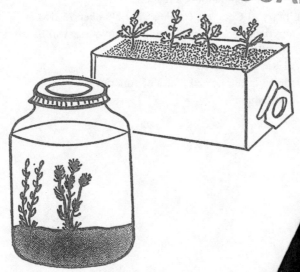

GEORGE I. SCHWARTZ
and BERNICE S. SCHWARTZ

DOUBLEDAY & COMPANY, INC.
Garden City, New York   1974

ISBN: 0-385-03357-5 Trade
      0-385-08000-x Prebound
Library of Congress Catalog Card Number 73–15171
Copyright © 1974 by GEORGE I. SCHWARTZ AND BERNICE S.
  SCHWARTZ
All Rights Reserved
Printed in the United States of America
First Edition

CONTENTS

PREFACE

You are the ecologist; this book was written for you. It will have succeeded if it stimulates you to participate by actively exploring and investigating the familiar world in which you live rather than to observe it passively. The young experimenter is challenged only when the problems presented are on his level of ability and offer him some chance of success.

This is a know-how book and it includes many experiments that require the building of equipment for some aspects of the investigations. We hope that the young experimenter will be encouraged to design, build, and improvise other devices to meet his needs in experiments he designs.

Along with the experiments, investigations, and explorations included here, the main interrelationships of living things and the environments that support them are developed as a primer of ecology. Theory and practice are brought together, as ecology is seen as a science that relates to our everyday lives.

In a number of the experiments we have inserted many questions to direct and strengthen observations. These questions are the kind that should be passing through the mind of any observer as he is absorbed with the functioning of the living world. The ability to ask the right questions is one key to success in all investigation.

As you spend more time in field studies and explorations, you will find your senses sharpened, your ability to observe improved, and your questions increasingly perceptive. You have learned to look at the world around you as an ecologist.

GEORGE I. SCHWARTZ
BERNICE S. SCHWARTZ

FOOD CHAINS AND ECOSYSTEMS

1 | A Way of Learning About the World of Life

Why learn ecology? Everyone is curious about the world in which he lives. This is especially true of the young. When we are young every experience is a new one. Each experience brings information. It might also be puzzling. Early in life we learn to ask questions about our experiences. Often the answers do not seem right. For some, this is very discouraging. However, many people never lose their curiosity and inquisitiveness about the world around them. When answers are unsatisfactory they continue to search and ask new questions. One reason is that for most of us there is a compelling need to know and to understand.

There are many ways of asking questions and finding out. Ecology is a fairly new science and it has developed techniques and procedures for asking questions about the living world. You will be introduced to many of the ways of ecology and will apply them to questions you want to ask about living things and their ways. This you will do by learning something about ecology as a science and about the nature and potential of science as you use its techniques in conducting your own investigations.

Ecology is the science that deals with the entire world of living things and its relations with the many environments in which they live. It also includes the relationships of living things with one another. It is part of the science of biology, the study of living things.

What we call ecology today was once called natural history. For a long time, natural history was descriptive only and did not use experimental techniques. Its discoveries were made by exploration and observations. There were some remarkable observers and there were others who let their imaginations run wild.

When biologists studying natural history began to emphasize the relationships between living things in particular environments and the real nature of the environment itself, they were introducing science into their approach. The individual living thing now represents a population of all others like itself. The biologist introduced mathematics and measurement into his studies as well as physics, chemistry, and geology. All these influences contributed to the newly emerging science of ecology.

Observation is no less important in ecology today than it was in natural history. But it is not the only way in which information is obtained, theories established, and laws recognized. By going out into forests, meadows, marshes, and ponds, the ecologist sees and recognizes problems and asks the questions which might lead him to studies and investigations he can pursue.

Carefully designed experiments, set up and conducted in the field or performed in a laboratory with living things collected in the field, are also utilized in solving problems. Others involve precise chemical and physical procedures, techniques, and equipment.

You, as a young investigator, can undertake some explorations in ecology. These include observation alone as well as a combination of observation and experiment. You can learn to use many of the techniques, procedures, and instruments used by ecologists. Above all, you can develop the ability to recognize problems, to ask meaningful questions, and to design investigations that will provide some answers and resolve some problems.

Ecology, then, is an outdoor science. It brings the great pleasure, joy, and excitement that being and working outdoors can. It also includes some responsibilities. When you go out into the field to explore a pond, a stream, a tide pool, or a beach, you will come to both public and private property. There are regulations that apply to the use of public lands. They are usually posted. But most such lands are available for reasonable use.

The owners of private property have the right to expect that their lands also will be respected. If you are able to, it is a good idea to get permission to enter and use private property for some of your explorations. It will help if you explain your purpose and just what you will do. If you are not able to get permission, do not enter the property. There are likely to be public areas that will meet your needs.

Collecting specimens is not the major goal of ecological studies. Most observations of the living world do not demand that specimens be gathered. A sketch, a drawing, or a photograph is excellent as an appropriate record. Many plants and animals are relatively rare and may be protected. This means that not a single specimen is to be taken. When you may, and do, collect, be sure not to overcollect. Some of the investigations in the chapters that follow include instructions for the kinds of collecting that are permitted.

Most of the equipment, materials, and apparatus required are simple, easy to make or obtain, and not expensive to buy. Sources of the things that must be purchased are listed in Appendix III. Kitchen, storage basement, and attic are sources of treasures that can be used, as is or improvised, to make equipment you can use. Such chemicals as are needed are few in number and easy to obtain.

A.   EQUIPMENT TO PURCHASE. You will make frequent use of a good 10- or 15-power folding hand lens; a good penknife; a flashlight; a tape measure; a number of plastic or glass vials or jars with screw caps; a knapsack with a shoulder strap; a camera (?); a small loose-leaf notebook; and a ball-point pen. These are the things you will generally take with you on every field visit.

B.   EQUIPMENT THAT CAN BE MADE. You may not want to make all the devices described in the balance of the book. Others you may design yourself and build for some special investigative purpose. The following equipment is easy to make and the materials needed to make them are generally available without special purchase. Included are observation boxes, rearing cages, pitfall and cover traps, quadrats, microquadrats, lantern-slide aquaria, plankton nets, Secchi discs, pooters, dragnets, and waterscopes.

C.   SUPPLIES FOUND AROUND THE HOUSE. There are many things that accumulate in homes that can be used in producing simple equipment for collecting and experimenting. These include many kinds of plastic and glass containers. Some utensils can be adapted for use. Several sizes of plastic bags as well as glass and plastic jars with covers can be used to carry fresh, salt water, and soil collections. Gallon, half-gallon, and quart-size widemouthed jars make good aquaria and terraria. One-pound and half-pound peanut butter jars are good as miniaquaria for small pond life. Shallow white enamel pans or plastic margarine containers are excellent for sorting out pond and marine collections.

Rubber bands of all sizes, twine, cord, wire clothes hangers, copper or brass wire, old screening (especially plastic screens), discarded funnels, cardboard of various sizes, Scotch tape, aluminum foil, glass panes, and boxes are all useful in improvising equipment. If the need arises for other things you will probably find them at home.

The joy and excitement of ecological studies are to be found in the field. It is here that the world of life reveals itself. But sometimes it conceals its patterns and structure. Some animals move around and are visible while others remain hidden as they carry on their life activities. The plants are always in place and they will be seen if you look carefully. Every visit also has its surprises. New animals and plants appear; new aspects of relationships within a community become evident. You think of questions as some of the things you see puzzle you. You begin to recognize that there are things to investigate and that you can approach them on your level of understanding. They are within your ability to explore with some chance of success. These will give you the background you need to move on to more specialized kinds of studies.

Plan all your visits to the field carefully. Know what you are looking for. State the purpose of each trip in your field notebook: "To explore the school grounds," or "To observe the insects in a vacant lot," or "To study the animals in a tide pool at the shore." When you make your visits you may be confused at first. You may not be able to identify the animals and plants you see. Don't be discouraged. Use simple names such as insect, beetle, butterfly, grasshopper, moss, fern, fungus, grass, or tree at first. As you meet them again and again, you will begin to know them more precisely as wolf spider, red maple tree, and inky cap mushroom. There are many ways of finding out the exact names and these will be introduced in the individual investigations. But the names and identification of living things should help us and not master us.

For safety it is always wise to have a friend along on all trips. The buddy system works as well on field trips as it does at the waterfront or in the swimming pool. Hazards are no more likely than they are anywhere else, but they are likely to be different. Thus, they cannot always be anticipated. With some one along, the problems will be minimized.

You must learn to recognize and avoid the few plants and animals of your area that are likely to cause problems. Two closely related plants are the major problem in many parts of the United States. They are poison ivy and poison sumac. Each produces an oil in every plant structure—leaf, stem, root, flowers, and the lead-white berries they each form. The oil is a contact poison. It irritates the skin and forms blisters wherever the oil touches the skin. The blisters appear about 24 hours after contact. Both plants should be avoided.

Figure 1.   Poison ivy.

Poison ivy (Figure 1) is the smaller of the two plants. It usually grows close to the ground, but it sometimes grows as a vine and, by using trees as a support, it grows to heights of 40 or more feet above the ground. The climbing stem is stout and is covered with tiny brown rootlets which can take in water from the air. Poison ivy thrives in all kinds of situations in every part of the United States.

Poison sumac (Figure 2) is a tall tree or shrub that reaches heights of 30 feet in swamps and on the margins of swamps from Maine to Florida and as far west as Minnesota, Missouri, and Louisiana. Its effects on the skin are the same as those of poison ivy but much more severe. Some of the names by which it is known tell us enough about it. In different areas it is called thunderwood, poisonwood, poison dogwood, poison ash, and poison elder.

Learn to recognize both these plants in winter as well as in the summer. The oil they produce is present at all times, so they can produce their irritation even when no leaves can be seen. The oil is

Figure 2.   Poison sumac.

transferred from plant to man by contact—it must be touched. Burning the plants to get rid of them is very risky. The heat of the burning evaporates the oil and the tiny droplets of oil are in the smoke given off. Walking through the smoke will bring thousands of small drops of oil in contact with exposed parts of the skin. Even worse is the effect of the oil on the lung surfaces if any smoke is inhaled. Enough said.

If you know or think you have had contact with poison ivy, the best treatment is to wash the affected parts with hot water (as hot as you can stand) and laundry soap (the strong, yellow bars). If you are in the field and do not have soap with you, use black pond mud to rub over the skin. Some people think they have immunity to poison ivy. The immunity is a relative reaction—there is an amount of exposure that will produce the irritation in everyone.

The potentially dangerous animals include a number of snakes, a few types of spiders and several scorpions. Each produces poisonous secretions which are injected as the animals strike, bite, or sting. Coral snakes, water moccasins, copperheads, and rattlesnakes are the poisonous snakes found in some areas of the United States. Check with a local museum or zoo or with your state conservation department to find out which of these snakes are found in the area in which you live.

It is possible to be in the field every day for weeks on end and not see a single snake. If you do come across one, the snake will retreat to avoid contact if it can possibly do so. There is even less chance that a poisonous snake will be encountered. In the remote possibility of a meeting, it is best to allow the snake to escape. When you explore areas in which snakes are common, remember where you are. Be alert to their possible presence and proceed cautiously.

Wear appropriate clothing, including leather boots or hiking shoes. If you do any climbing, watch where you place your hands. Turn over logs or stones with a long stick. Do not reach under rocky ledges where you cannot see. Stay on paths and trails. Most instances of snake bite are the result of amateurs becoming careless as they handle poisonous snakes.

Scorpions are found in dry, warm climates. They are usually active at night when they move about and feed. They often are found under rocks and stones during daylight hours. They do not attack but sting in self-defense. The sting organ is found at the end of the long tail. The poison is injected by a whipping action in which the tail is quickly moved forward. Most stings are not dangerous, but they can be quite painful.

Two types of spiders are known to be poisonous. These are the female black widow and the brown recluse spiders. The black widow is found in many warm areas while its relatives are found throughout much of America.

The brown recluse spider is smaller and is commonly found in houses in the southwestern United States. It is best to know these animals, to be able to recognize them quickly, and to avoid them. There are excellent color drawings of the poisonous snakes, spiders, and scorpions in two of the reference books listed in the appendix: the Golden Nature guides on spiders and on reptiles and amphibians.

Keeping and maintaining a good notebook of your ecological work is important in establishing an accurate record of your work. You might find it desirable to use two notebooks: a smaller field notebook which you carry with you on all field trips and a larger permanent notebook which you keep at home.

The field book should be a loose-leaf book with a soft, plastic cover which measures about $6\frac{3}{4} \times 3\frac{3}{4}$ inches. It fits in the pocket and is easy to carry. Entries made in this notebook are original observations, and you should include all data required to produce a complete record.

Every trip should carry the date, the weather and air temperature, and the time of day when observations are recorded. Do not depend on your memory; record all data.

When you have time at home, record the notes in the permanent notebook. This can be a bound notebook or a loose-leaf book about 8×10 inches or larger. The transfer of notes should be done carefully and checked before the original field notes are discarded. You may want to include maps, sketches, drawings, or photographs if these are part of the original record.

Often in the course of working in the field you will see things you want to record in ways other than with words. Pencil sketching is a useful and rewarding method of recording observations. You do not have to be an artist to make acceptable and attractive sketches. When you begin to sketch you will find yourself observing more closely and accurately as you try to record a scene. You can make your sketches in your field notebook and do not have to carry additional equipment and materials with you. The sketches in this book were made in the field, and they suggest several approaches to this method of making records of observations.

Photography is another tool available for recording observations. If you do not have a camera, it is not necessary to buy one. Cameras are so common that it is unlikely that you cannot get one to use from time to time.

If the camera available is a Polaroid, then you can have your photographs a minute or less after you make the exposure. While Polaroid film is more expensive than conventional film, you do know immediately whether your photo record is usable. You will learn to be selective in the pictures you take and thus keep the cost relatively low.

Hundreds of other types of cameras are available and more than a few are quite inexpensive. Every one of them will produce good photos if you learn to use them. This is not difficult since each camera comes with a good instruction manual. There are some good, inexpensive books on photography, including a few on nature photography listed in Appendix II.

Comfort and safety should both be considered in dressing for field trips. The weather and the season will determine the weight and type of clothes to wear. Arms and legs should be covered to protect them from brambles and other thorny plants. A sweater or jacket with pockets to carry smaller things is good for cooler weather while rainwear is necessary on rainy days. Yes, fieldworkers go out, rain or shine.

Appropriate and comfortable shoes are a must. If you intend to visit marshy or swampy ground, pond or ocean shore, waterproof shoes or boots are essential. Carry an extra pair of socks whenever you go into wet areas.

Many insects can be a nuisance in spring and summer, especially near wet areas. Mosquitos, midges, flies, and their relatives are both pesky and annoying. An insect repellent such as 611 rubbed over hands, arms, and face helps keep most of them away from you. We have found that Johnson's Baby Oil used in the same way is just as effective.

The Language of Ecology.   Much of the vocabulary comes from biology. Many other terms are words from our common everyday speech. For ecological use they have been given a sharper, more precise meaning. It has also developed its own special vocabulary. The meaning of a number of the more important terms is given below.

ATMOSPHERE—The envelope of gases in contact with the surface of all waters and with the land areas of the earth. It consists mainly of nitrogen and oxygen with smaller amounts of carbon dioxide and a number of rare gases. It also contains water vapor which forms clouds and falls as rain, hail, or snow.

BIOGEOCHEMICAL CYCLE—The circulation of a number of chemicals through an ecosystem. These chemicals are part of the atmosphere, the soil, and the waters of the earth, and they are used by the living things of the ecosystem in their activities. Ultimately they are returned to the environment from the wastes and the bodies of the plants and animals.

BIOSPHERE—All the parts of the earth that support life make up the biosphere.

CARNIVORE—A consumer organism which eats flesh. Lions and tigers are carnivores.

COMMUNITY—All the living things that live in a particular environment and that interact with one another.

CONSUMER—A living thing that cannot make its own food and must get it ready-made from other living things.

COMPETITION—The demand by two or more organisms for the same limited supply of food, water, minerals, and a place in the sun.

DECOMPOSER—A living thing that feeds on the wastes and bodies of other living things in its environment. Bacteria and fungi are the main decomposers.

DOMINANT—The most common and characteristic type of plant in a particular plant community. Thus the oak trees are dominants in an oak-hickory forest and Queen Anne's lace is the dominant in an open field in the northeastern United States.

ECOLOGICAL NICHE—The specific job of a particular kind of living thing in the ecosystem of which it is a part. Thus the green plants are all producers in most communities while the deer or mountain lion are consumers.

ECOLOGICAL SUCCESSION—Many communities are not stable but go through stages in which some species of plants and animals disappear and others become prominent. There is eventually a stable community in which the living things are in balance. This is called a *climax community*.

ECOSYSTEM—The combination of all the living things in a community and the environment which supports them and with which they interact.

FOOD CHAIN—The chain of living things in a community in which each link in the chain feeds on a link below it and is fed upon by the one above it. In most communities the living things may be part of more than one chain and the chains are linked in a more intricate *food web*.

HABITAT—The environment part of an ecosystem in which the community lives. A pond is a habitat as is a stream and a marsh.

HERBIVORE—A consumer that feeds on plant matter. A deer is a herbivore; so is a grasshopper.

HOST—The living thing whose body provides food for an invading parasite. The water turtle is the host to a turtle leech which attaches itself to the skin of the turtle and extracts blood on which it feeds.

HYDROSPHERE—All the waters, fresh and salt, that cover 70 per cent of the earth's surface.

LITHOSPHERE—The solid part of the earth including the core, the crust which includes all the rocks we can observe directly, and the mantle which lies between the crust and the core.

PARASITE—A living thing that lives in or on the body of a living thing of a different type from which it extracts all its nourishment.

POPULATION—All the individuals of a particular type of living thing that live in one ecosystem. All the red oaks in an oak forest or all the smallmouth bass in a lake make up populations.

PREDATOR-PREY—A predator is an animal that feeds on another animal, its prey. The predator-prey relationship is part of a food chain. Thus in Africa the lion is the predator and the zebra is its prey.

PRODUCER—Any living thing able to make its own food from simple chemicals. The green plants are the producers of the earth and support all other life on the earth.

REDUCER—A living thing that feeds on wastes and the dead bodies of living things; decomposers and scavengers are reducers.

SYMBIOSIS—The relationship between two different types of living things in which each benefits. A termite cannot digest wood but the tiny organisms that live in its intestine can. The termite chews and takes in wood while the microbes in its intestine digest it in the moist, protected environment of the termite's gut.

No science can develop without a strong mathematical base. Ecology is no exception. Description is not enough to exploit the power of the scientific method. It is necessary to measure and to count, to extract meaning from the results of experiments.

Do not become alarmed by the suggestion that you will be immersed in mathematical ideas. You will not have to understand the theory that underlies the mathematics used here. You will be introduced to an interesting mathematical technique that is very productive in ecology. It is also used in advertising, politics, insurance, economics, manufacturing, and many other areas of human interest. It will enable you to understand what numbers tell you. This you can do without being a mathematician.

As you explore woods and fields, you cannot help being impressed by the things you observe. There are so many kinds of plants and animals, even in a small area. They vary in a number of ways that you can easily see. You may decide that they probably vary in ways that are not obvious. No two green frogs, or horseshoe crabs, or water fleas, or cinnamon ferns, or red maple trees are alike. We are constantly reminded of variation in the world of life.

Living things of the same type differ in height or weight or in color or pattern or in many other qualities that can be measured. How would you determine the height of the average red maple tree in a wooded area? It is not difficult to make a fairly accurate estimate of the height of one tree. Should you measure the height of all the red maples you can find and then calculate the average? Suppose when you check you are told that there are about one thousand red maples in the wood. Do you really have to measure all the trees? Also, how accurate is the estimate of a thousand-tree population for the total? Did someone count every mature tree? Did he include the younger trees, not yet fully grown?

There are ways of determining the number of trees in a habitat or the height of any type of tree or the number of earthworms in the soil or any other type of information you require without looking at every single one. These methods are called sampling, and they are used often in ecological work as in many other disciplines. A sample is a small part of the whole population used to represent the entire population.

Taking a sample of plants which do not move about is different than getting a sample of animals which move about. The purpose is the same. It is to discover something about a whole population by examining a small part of that population. If the sample is well selected, sampling works. Sample polls of voters in an election predict with surprising accuracy how the whole voting population will vote. Carefully checking a sample of some manufactured article for defective ones will indicate how many defective items will probably occur in the whole output.

A few investigations using sampling techniques are suggested in the chapters that follow. You will not need to work with complicated mathematics to do them. But you will probably appreciate how it is possible to reach answers of reasonable accuracy without unreasonable work.

2 | Living Things: Their Needs and Interrelations

This earth of ours has supported life for about two billion years. When living things first appeared on the earth, they found conditions in which they could survive and thrive. The sun's rays poured down on the earth without fail. The temperatures were neither too high nor too low. Water, carbon dioxide, oxygen, minerals, and the other chemicals that living things need to stay alive were available in adequate amounts. Since the conditions and substances needed by living things were present over long periods of time, they prospered.

In this long span of time, individual living things died, but they left offspring to continue the race. Many races and types also vanished from the earth. But new races and types constantly appeared, replaced them, and flourished. The stream of life was destined to continue even though the cast of characters changed.

The earth also changed following the first appearance of life. Sometimes the changes were sudden and violent, as in an earthquake or the eruption of a volcano. More often the changes were gradual and slow. Land areas were built up or worn away by waves, river currents, tides, ice, rain and sandstorms, as well as by the actions of the living plants and animals. Some land areas were invaded by the seas and submerged; while other land masses were created when giant forces pushed their surfaces above the water's level.

The earth as we know it today is the product of its long past. So, too, is the living world. It consists of tremendous populations of a million or more different varieties of animals as well as about three hundred thousand kinds of plants alive today. This vast array of living things is impressive evidence of the fitness of the earth to support life as well as the fitness of living things to survive in the environments provided by the earth.

The surface of the earth is also varied and it provides many special environments in which living things prosper. Water covers close to three fourths of the earth's surface. In the forms of oceans, seas, bays, lakes, rivers, streams, ponds and swamps, it provides watery homes or habitats for a range of organisms so small that they can be seen only with a microscope. It also is home for the largest animal ever to live on the earth, the giant sulphur-bottom whale. The microscopic living things make up in numbers what they lack in size. They feed not only the huge whales, but also all the smaller animals that fill the earth's waters with life.

The land surfaces of the earth are even more varied as habitats than are salt and fresh waters. Deserts, forests, meadows, fields, prairies, mountains, and numberless other land situations are each associated with unique communities of living things which interact with each other as well as with the environment. Thus, the desert habitats of the western United States feature cactuses large and small, along with many unusual plants such as the Ocatillo, the palo verde tree, mesquite, the creosote bush, and, at times, thousands of small but beautifully flowered plants. Animals of the desert might include scorpions, tarantulas, rattlesnakes, lizards, cactus wrens, elf owls, road runners, insects, and many other unusual types.

There is much more to the desert community than the plants and animals likely to be found in it. Why are these living things found in a desert and not in a forest, a meadow, or on a beach? Obviously the conditions of existence in a desert differ from those found in forests, meadows, or in other land environments. How can we explain the wide spacing of plants in the desert with the way in which the plants in a field or meadow or forest grow? How are the plants in each habitat equipped to survive in their own habitat and not in others?

The climate differs as does the weather. The amounts of rainfall and of sunshine are different as are the soil and the kinds and amounts of minerals in the soil. At the same time, the plants and animals found in a desert habitat or any other habitat are there because they are adapted to its special conditions and to each other. Within each habitat there are patterns in the relationships as well as rhythms of the life. The living things influence the physical environment and are in turn affected by it.

The science of ecology is the study of these relationships and their rhythms and patterns. It is this that calls us to explore and to discover, for we are part of this world of life and everything in it. We can learn to read the landscape and to interpret the condition of the environment and the living things it supports. We can look for signs of change and understand how they might affect the life of the community or the environment.

It is not necessary to travel to far-off places to be an ecologist and to investigate ecological questions. The vacant lot near home, a small pond you pass on the way to school, or the school grounds themselves can be utilized as you participate in ecological discovery. You can make some of the equipment you need; other items can be obtained without too much difficulty or expense. How does an ecologist go about his work? Let us look at some examples of ecologists in action.

The ecologist looks for and tries to understand what goes on in natural communities. He spends much time in exploring natural areas wherever he can. Part of some investigations can be conducted in laboratories, but field exploration is basic to his work. His training and experience prepare him to recognize problems. When he has identified a problem he selects a limited aspect for investigation. He then tries to state the problem sharply and precisely. He designs his experiments and often makes the equipment needed. He asks efficient questions and devises effective ways of getting answers to them. He keeps careful records and checks his results to be sure that he has made no errors in developing his inquiry.

The field is more than a laboratory for the ecologist. It is often the source of his ideas, particularly when he is not working on an investigation. As he visits familiar habitats, or new ones, he is alert to the appearance of a new pattern; an alteration of a rhythm; or a plant or animal surviving in an unexpected place. Let us walk along with an ecologist as he returns for his weekly look at the edge of a marsh and the adjoining fields and wooded area.

It is late in July, and this is just an exploratory trip. The first objective is to find some evening primroses, a weedlike plant that grows in dry or sandy soil. It produces attractive yellow flowers about this time of the year. The ecologist has been told about an unusual moth that is associated with the flower. He hopes he can find some and photograph them.

The moth he is looking for flies at night and moves from flower to flower. During the day it hides in the flower whose petals are partially closed. He looked at thirty or forty flowers before he found his first moth.

The moth is very attractive with unusually colored wings. The forward portion is bright pink or rosy red while the back part of the wing is pale yellow and closely matches the color of the petals. The moth rests during the day and is not easy to see, since only the yellow wing tips are visible. In old flowers the petals begin to turn pink and the wing color helps to conceal the moth within.

As the moth moves from flower to flower it carries pollen and makes certain the cross pollination necessary for the production of seeds. The seeds will produce the next year's evening primroses. The females lay their eggs near the buds of new flowers and the bright green caterpillars (larvae) feed on the petals of the flower and grow rapidly. They finally enter a part of the bud where they are transformed into pupae which spend the winter in the seed capsule.

Many more visits during the next few months will be required to see and photograph the remaining stages in the life cycle. The ecologist makes entries in the field notebook he always carries with him. In a morning of searching he found only eight adult moths and saw no signs of egg laying. The evening primroses he was studying were very tall—over six feet in height. He noted in his field notes that this warranted some investigation since most of the varieties in his area were somewhat shorter. He remembered that in an earlier visit he had seen a good collection of the plants growing alongside the road about a quarter of a mile away.

On reaching the new site he found many flowers in bloom, but no moths. In his field book, a note with a question mark indicates his interest in possibly trying to find out why. Something else caught his eye. A small stand of milkweed plants at the edge of the road had been invaded by a horde of caterpillars which were fiercely chewing up the leaves of the plant. They were the strangest-looking caterpillars he had ever seen.

Each larva was covered with long tufts of orange, black, and white hairs. One plant had eight caterpillars on a single leaf, and it looked as though it was covered with a miniature hooked rug. They were efficient feeders and completely devoured the leaf in about 15 minutes. They moved on to another leaf. Their food intake was so great it almost seemed that you could see them grow. Another entry in the field notebook carried the notation that this might lead to some later investigations.

Before the day was over, this small area provided many provocative observations that might lead to studies in the future. Two female wolf spiders were found under two separate rocks. One was dragging an attached egg case about the size of a pea. The second one was carrying an empty case while the newly emerged young spiders—about 100 strong—rode on her back. She looked as though she was wearing a fur coat. As the two animals were being photographed, the young spiders left their mother's back and scurried away. They were seen later to find their way back and climb aboard again.

Four other rocks, when turned over, yielded four young snakes; three garter snakes and a black racer. One of the young garters was devouring a tiny toad. The rocks also yielded an assortment of centipedes, pill bugs, slugs, beetles, and ants. It was a good day for looking. Reflection later suggested a number of future projects.

For a long time the earth could not support life. The combination of conditions and materials needed was missing. Somehow, when everything required was available life appeared, and the procession of life on the earth was on its way. It is possible to look back and to use what is known today to determine just what it is that supports and maintains life.

The physical environment yielded many of its secrets to the questions and investigations of many scientists, especially in the last hundred years. You, too, can observe and study local environments in a search for answers to your own questions. Why do certain plants grow in one plot of land and not in what looks like a similar plot close to it? Why is the floor of a pine forest so bare of ground cover while that of a maple or oak-hickory is so rich in shrubs, vines, and small nonwoody plants?

Living things exist on the earth because they have a source of available energy. This energy enables them to grow, to reproduce their own kind, to move, and to carry out all those activities we recognize as living. The automobiles, airplanes, tractors, motors, and other machines used by man cannot perform without energy; neither can man nor any other living thing.

The source of all energy on the earth is the sun, whose light pours down ceaselessly, as it has for billions of years. The energy is released by a chemical reaction in the sun and is radiated out into space in all directions. That part of the sun's rays that reaches the earth has many effects.

The surface of the earth is heated by the rays. Land areas are thus warmed. The temperature of the air in contact with the land is also raised. Since different areas of the earth are heated differently, the air is set in motion by the warming and produces many of the effects we call weather. The earth's waters are also heated and the sun's energy contributes to the evaporation of much water from the surface of bodies of water. The water vapor formed gives rise to clouds that ultimately return the water to the surface in the form of rain, snow, and hail.

The effect of the sun's rays on green plants is immediately vital to life, since it is the way that energy from the sun is introduced into the world of life. Green plants serve as energy traps. They convert the energy from sunlight into stored chemical energy in the process of photosynthesis.

Photosynthesis is the process by which green plants use water and the gas, carbon dioxide, to produce a simple sugar. Sugar is a carbohydrate, as is starch. These are energy-rich chemicals, and they are found in all plants and animals. The energy in the sugar was converted by the plant from the sun's energy to something it can use, as can every kind of living thing.

Since the bodies of all living things contain proteins, oils, and fats and carbohydrates other than sugar, these, too, must be made. They are produced by green plants from the sugar and whatever other chemical are needed. The energy required for this bigger job is obtained by using some of the sugar made by photosynthesis.

Animals cannot utilize the sun's energy to make energy-rich chemicals. They must take in the foods which contain proteins, carbohydrates, and fats as their energy source. They are thus directly or indirectly feeding upon plants. They are able to extract the stored chemical energy in their food and convert it into the energy that keeps them going.

Animals release the energy in the foods they take in by burning it in the process called respiration. They need the gas, oxygen, to perform this life-sustaining process. The atmosphere contains about 20 per cent oxygen which also takes part in all burning and other combustion that occurs in the non-living world. Plants as well as animals need oxygen for their respiration as they perform all their life activities, except photosynthesis which uses energy from the sun.

Plants and animals that live in water get their oxygen from the water. Oxygen dissolves in water and the supply of this essential chemical is maintained at the surface where the water is in contact with the atmosphere.

Nitrogen, another gas, makes up about 78 per cent of the atmosphere while the rest of the air includes a number of gases in slight amounts. The most important of these gases to life on the earth is carbon dioxide—one raw material needed for photosynthesis.

Life began in water, and for at least a billion years, it was limited to water. Water is a very stable environment since its temperature and other physical qualities vary little. Nothing similar to weather or climate exists below the surface. The light needed for photosynthesis reaches depths of up to 100 feet, which enables plants to function to that point. Animals are able to move to even greater depths.

Living things finally moved onto the land and were soon established there. Any area with conditions suitable for life was ultimately colonized. The major feature of land surfaces is the soil, a mixture of mineral particles such as sand, silt, and clay, dissolved minerals, water, and some organic matter (decaying and decayed plant and animal substances). Weathering of the rocks making up the surface of the earth gradually produced the particles of sand, silt, and clay.

Water kept falling in the form of rain or snow and contributed minerals dissolved from the rocks and particles. The early plants that first colonized the land and those that followed died, and in their breakdown they provided the organic matter that distinguishes soils today.

Every living thing is thus surrounded by fluids (water or air) even those that live in the soil. Plants are anchored to the ground wherever they can obtain the substances they require to function. From the ground they absorb water, dissolved minerals, and oxygen, while the air that surrounds the parts above ground supplies both oxygen and carbon dioxide. Sunlight is generally available while seasonal and climatic changes produce wide ranges of temperature as well as the amount of water available.

Most living things do well in the temperature range between 20° and 100° F. There are some simple living things such as bacteria and blue-green algae that can tolerate the temperature of hot springs, about 212° F., while many bacteria are not damaged by temperatures far below the freezing point of water. These are extremes; the majority of living things thrive at optimal temperatures somewhere between the freezing point and the boiling point of water.

In addition to its role in photosynthesis, radiation from the sun also plays its part in maintaining the temperature of the environment. Its heat warms the waters of the earth and the land surfaces. The air in contact with water and land surfaces is also heated by contact, and the resulting air movements contribute to winds and other atmospheric effects we call weather. Through the seasons, the changes in weather are responsible for the climate of an area.

Solar radiation also plays a part in cycling water, through the evaporation of water to give rise to clouds and the fall of the moisture in clouds as rain and snow in other parts of the earth. These water movements are also part of the patterns of weather.

A number of chemical substances are essential to living things. Oxygen and carbon dioxide have already been mentioned. The group of substances we call food are in this group of necessary materials. The proteins, fats, and carbohydrates that all living things must have are composed of carbon along with hydrogen and oxygen. Proteins also include nitrogen, sulfur, and sometimes phosphorus. Each of these chemical elements is found in soils and in water in the form of mineral salts which dissolve readily in moisture.

There are other chemical elements which living things need in tiny amounts. These include silicon, copper, magnesium, and a few others which also are to be found in soils, in many rocks and other bodies found in the surface, and in the waters covering the earth.

Plants are especially sensitive to even small differences in the amounts of many of these substances in the soil, and this helps to explain why the same kind of plants will not be found growing in two plots of land that lie next to each other.

Finally, the most plentiful chemical compound on the earth, water. We have already noted water as a feature of the environment of living things. It is also a major substance vital to the existence of life. It makes up the fluids of all living things and is one raw material with which plants carry on photosynthesis. The life-supporting activities in all living things occur in watery solutions. Water is a simple chemical compound. It is composed of two atoms of hydrogen combined with a single atom of oxygen. It has unique properties that fit it for its many roles in living activities.

Ecology is a practical science. Its subject matter, the world of life, lends itself to experiment. Wherever we live we can reach a variety of habitats which support communities of living things. Each habitat can provide opportunities for observation, investigation, and experiment. Questions and problems abound. The equipment needed to study them is simple.

It is not possible to include here all the questions and problems that might be investigated. There will, however, be opportunity to learn how to recognize problems and then to design the procedures to solve them. It will include the making of apparatus and learning how to use it. Above all it will introduce you, the young ecologist, to the joy, the fun, and the wonder of investigating the world of life.

EXPERIMENT 1. To Measure Some Properties of Soils.

Materials and Equipment. Hand trowel; frozen-juice cans with top and bottom removed; widemouthed glass jars (pint and quart sizes); plastic or metal funnel; pH paper (see Appendix III); thermometer; large metal cans with tops removed; field notebook.

A. pH of the Soil. Soils vary in their chemical make-up. We can see the results in the different kinds of plants that grow in different soils. pH is fairly easy to measure. The term pH describes how acid or alkaline a fluid or liquid is. When the pH of the soil is measured, the soil's water is used to make the determination.

pH values are expressed with a scale of numbers from 0 to 14 (Figure 3). A pH of 0 is extremely acid; 1 is less; and 2 is still less; up to a pH of 7 which is *neutral*. Numbers above 7 mark alkaline conditions, with 14 the most alkaline. Soils generally show pH ranging from 3.5 to 11, with some showing a greater range.

pH is often measured by chemicals called indicators. The indicators used show the pH by a change in color. The most common indicator which you probably know is litmus. Litmus turns red in acid liquids

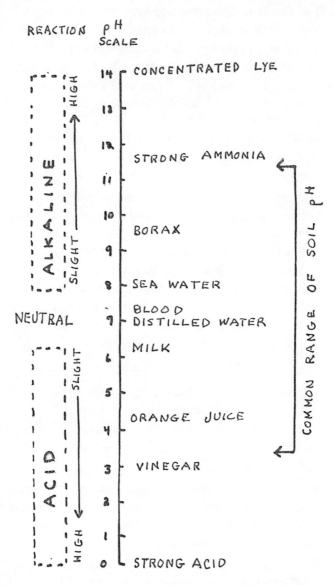

Figure 3. The pH scale and some common substances with their pH values.

and blue when the liquid is alkaline. Litmus solution can be soaked up by absorbent papers, such as filter paper, and dried. Red litmus paper is used to test fluids that are thought to be alkaline, and blue litmus paper is used for acid liquids. Other indicators have been developed which are sensitive to narrow or wide ranges of pH. They show by distinct colors the specific pH which they measure.

Hydrion pH papers are supplied in rolls that also include a color chart which can be used to read the pH of any material being tested. One maker provides a paper sensitive to the pH range of 1–12. A roll with dispenser and color chart for 100 tests costs a little more than one dollar.

Collect small samples of a series of soils from different locations such as a field, the floor of a woods and the edge of a swamp, or any other areas available to you. Use a small trowel and dig out a small section about 3 inches deep. Put each type of soil in a separate plastic bag along with a small piece of paper with the soil type and its location.

Cut six 1-inch sections of hydrion paper and moisten each with tap water. Place the strips on a sheet of wax paper and put a large pinch of soil from the top of each soil type on the wet hydrion strips. Add a few drops of water to each soil sample to moisten it.

Turn the wax paper over and lift the test strips from the soil. Check their color with the color chart and record the pH of each sample in your record book. Make a second series of tests with soil from the same sources, but take your soil from the bottom of the section. Do top and bottom layers of the soil samples have the same pH? Can you suggest why or why not?

Did you recognize any of the plants growing in the soils you tested? If you are interested in continuing this type of investigation, collect samples of soil in the same way from a number of other sources and determine their pH. Keep a record of any plants from these soils you can identify. Books on gardening and horticulture often carry information on the best pH range for growing many varieties of cultivated plants.

B. Water-holding Capacity of the Soil.   Soil is a major reservoir of water for plants and man. Its porous structure enables it to hold enormous quantities of water that fall as rain or snow. Soils differ in their ability to hold water. Good soils with their plant cover can absorb and hold much more water than can sandy soils.

Collect a number of soil samples of different quality: sandy soil; rich soil from the forest floor; soil with a high clay content; and any others available to you. Put each in a plastic bag with appropriate identification. When you return home, open the bags and allow the soils to air-dry fully before using.

Use small frozen-juice cans with both top and bottom covers removed. Cover one surface of each can with a double layer of gauze or cheesecloth. Use rubber bands or string to hold the cloth firmly in place. Carefully put enough soil of each type in a separate can until the can is three-fourths full. Make sure that the dry soil is loosely packed in each container.

Place one can with soil in a funnel which is resting in an empty glass vessel (jar) to collect the water that is not absorbed by the soil. Slowly pour one cup of water into the soil (Figure 4). The soil will absorb all

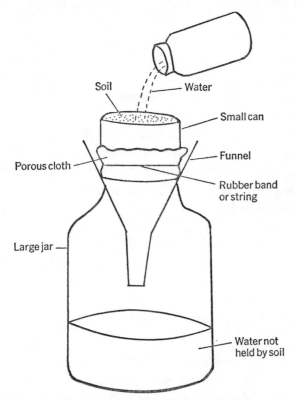

Figure 4.   Apparatus to measure the water-holding capacity of the soil.

it can hold. The rest will pass through the soil and into the collecting jar. When no more water passes through, measure the quantity of water that passes through into the cup. Record the amount.

Continue the same procedure with each sample of soil. Which soil had the best water-holding capacity? Which was poorest? Could you have predicted the result?

C. Soil Structure. Naturally formed soils have similar basic structure. This can be seen in profiles that are part of construction activities. An excavation more than five feet deep or a cut for a roadway extended through a hillside will provide a good view of a soil profile.

The relatively thin dark layer of topsoil lies above a lighter-colored subsoil. Below the two upper layers is one of bedrock, usually about five feet or more below the surface.

Take a small amount of material from each of the layers. Rub it between your fingers. How are the textures different? Which layer would hold water best? Use the technique described in Experiment 1B to determine the answer.

Another method of determining soil texture is to allow soil to settle in water. Use a one-quart screw-cap jar. Fill the jar to three fourths of its height with water. Add enough soil to raise the level of water so the jar is almost full. Tightly screw on the cap and shake the jar vigorously. Allow the jar to stand quietly until all the soil solids have settled (Figure 5).

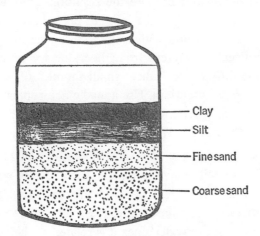

Figure 5. Separation of layers of material that make up a sample of soil. Other soils will show other layers and different thicknesses of the layers. Why do the layers separate this way?

Measure the depth of the different layers and record. Note that good topsoil consists of particles of fine sand, some clay, and humus, the name given to decayed organic matter. The structure, properties, and formation of soils beyond this simple introduction can be pursued in the books listed in the references in the appendix.

EXPERIMENT 2.   To Measure Some Properties of Pond Water.

Materials and Equipment.   Hydrion or other pH papers; Secchi disc; jars and other glass containers; thermometer; medicine droppers.

A. pH of Pond Water, Aquarium Water, and Swamp Water.   Water, both fresh and salt, serves as a major habitat for living things. Its chemical and physical properties determine the kinds of living things it will support. The waters that flow and drain into ponds and lakes contain chemicals dissolved as these waters flow through soils and over rocky surfaces. They also contain varying amounts of dissolved oxygen and carbon dioxide—both vital to life in the water. The dissolved materials in water affect its pH (relative acid or alkaline condition) as well as other properties. So do materials excreted by plants and animals. For these reasons it is often necessary to determine the pH of waters being studied.

Determine the pH of each sample of water collected with short 1½ inch strips of hydrion paper. Use a medicine dropper to place a small drop on the strip. Compare the resulting color with the color chart and record. How wide is the range of pH values?

If you have an aquarium with tropical fish measure the pH of its water. Is it noticeably different from the value for pond water? Can you explain the difference? Collect small samples of water from different depths in your aquarium. Use a medicine dropper to get a small amount of water at the 6-inch and 12-inch levels. Measure the pH. Did you expect the results? Why?

B. Temperature of Fresh Waters.   Temperatures of bodies of water vary, as do air and soil temperature. The variations in water are much smaller since water has great heat-holding capacity. This accounts for its much more stable temperature. It is important to determine the temperature of bodies of water since it is related to the activities of the living things in the water.

The precision and accuracy of temperature readings made with ordinary thermometers is limited, but they will suffice for your purposes. The type used in photography is good enough and quite inexpensive. Precision laboratory thermometers or electrical devices are too expensive to use even though they are more accurate.

Locate a section of the edge of a pond in which the surface or part of it is shaded by trees and shrubs. There will always be sunlit areas. Lower the bulb of a thermometer about 3 inches below the surface, and record the temperature in both a shaded and a lighted area. Try making additional readings at two-hour intervals from morning until dusk. Explain the results.

If the pond is from 3 to 5 feet deep, record temperatures at 2, 3, and 5 feet below the surface. Make a surface reading also, and record your results. Explain. Would the results be the same in a large lake in which you can lower the thermometer to a depth of 30 feet or more? If you can get the use of a small boat in a deep-water lake, make measurements at greater depths.

C. Light Penetration in Water. Light is essential to green plants wherever they live. The depth to which light penetrates bodies of water determines the level below which photosynthesis cannot occur. The nature of water; the chemicals usually dissolved in it; the quantity of microscopic plants and animals in the water; and the amount of suspended particles such as silt, soil, and others affect the penetration of light. A heavy rainfall will stir up small particles and often these do not completely settle for several days.

Light penetration is fairly easy to measure with a Secchi disc. This can be made from a circular disc of light metal, aluminum, or tin plate. It should be from 6 to 8 inches in diameter. Make a Secchi disc as shown in Figure 6. To make a Secchi disc you will need a circular metal disc, a large threaded eyebolt, 2 or 4 hexagonal nuts to fit the eyebolt, 20–30 feet of strong nylon line, small amounts of waterproof black and white paint.

a. Obtain a paint-can cover, an aluminum or other circular metal disc from 8 to 12 inches in diameter.

b. Drill a hole in the exact center of the disc large enough to contain the eyebolt.

c. Paint the surface of the disc, as shown in the illustration, with black and white waterproof paint. Allow to dry thoroughly.

d. Put 1 or 2 hexagonal nuts on the eyebolt as far as they will move on the threads. Insert the stem of the eyebolt through the center opening and fasten the eyebolt by adding 1 or 2 hexagonal nuts. The eyebolt and the nuts add enough weight for the disc to sink readily.

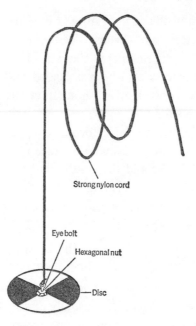

Strong nylon cord

Eye bolt

Hexagonal nut

—Disc

*Figure 6. A Secchi disc for measuring the depth to which light
penetrates a body of water.*

Use a 20-foot length of strong, light nylon cord to lower the disc in
water. Put a series of knots in the cord at 6-inch intervals to make the
measurement easy to read directly.

Secchi-disc readings should be made in deeper waters. This means
that a small boat will be required to reach the area of a pond or lake
where its waters are deep. In some places there may be a small pier
from the end of which some readings can be made. Lower the disc in
the water of the pond or lake until the disc is just visible. Note the
depth and allow the disc to move to a lower position where it cannot
be seen clearly. Slowly raise the disc until it is visible again. Record
the two depths and add the two numbers to determine the average by
dividing by two.

Take a series of pairs of readings in different areas of the body of
water you are examining. Determine average depths for each reading.
What is gained by making a number of readings? What does a reading
of 5 feet tell you about the water in a pond or lake? What would a
reading of 35 feet mean?

3 | The Relationships of Living Things

The living things on the earth are not scattered haphazardly over its surface. There is order and pattern in the world of life even though we may not recognize it at first. We must train ourselves to observe effectively so that we can recognize the role of different living things we see and the relationships of living things to the others in its environment. This is what is called reading the landscape.

It is this aspect of the life around us that will be developed in the chapters ahead. The investigations and experiments are intended to direct your viewing so that you see much more than you saw before. You will learn to ask effective questions and to design the ways in which you can find the answers to your questions. You will recognize different patterns of life within the broader ones you already understand. And you will have done much of it yourself.

The best way to begin is to explore those parts of the biosphere that you can find close to home. The word biosphere is used to describe all the parts of the earth surface in which life exists. It consists of forests and prairies; of ponds and streams; of oceans and seas; of beaches and deserts; and even of your own back yard. Each of these is a special environment in which some living things can survive. These are the habitats that support life. All the plants and animals that live in a particular habitat make up the community of that habitat.

The community plus the habitat that supports it is called an ecosystem. Thus, the pond ecosystem includes the plants large and small and all the animals that make the pond their home. It also includes some of the plants and animals of the surrounding land that interact with the pond community. Other ecosystems are found in deserts and meadows; in tide pools and in forests; and in almost every other kind of water or land environment.

In any ecosystem each living thing has contact with a number of other living things in the community. Each is also affected by the environment. The details of the relationships vary from community to community, but in every one it is possible to discover two distinct features: (1) there is a flow of energy from the sun through the green plants to animals that feed on green plants or on other animals; and (2) there is a movement of chemicals from the environment into the bodies of living things and then back to the environment. This cycling of chemicals between the living and the non-living world makes it possible for a relatively small supply of chemicals needed by the living world to go a long way. Living systems maintain themselves in very efficient ways.

Every living thing in a community has a job to do. We can often determine what that job or niche is by observing it, especially as it gets and uses food. The key living things in any community are the green plants both large and small. They are the *producers* for the living world. They initiate the flow of energy by trapping light energy from the sun to make food. The radiant energy is thus converted into the stored chemical energy in the plant's body.

The energy then moves into the animal world, as plant-eating animals (herbivores) play the part of first-level *consumers*. Whales, elephants, deer, and caterpillars are all herbivores since they are able to use plant materials to serve all their needs in growing, moving about, and doing all the other things active animals do.

This is the place where the meat eaters (carnivores) feed on the herbivores as second-level consumers. Small fish and large fish, foxes, dragonflies, swallows and owls are all carnivores. In some ecosystems there may be third- or even fourth-level consumers which are often larger than the second-level consumers.

The transfer of energy from the producers to the different levels of consumers is a food chain. A few simple food chains are shown below. Observation will enable you to trace out food chains as you visit different ecosystems. There are hundreds of food chains in the large ecosystems, and many of them include animals and plants in common. Some specific plants and animals may serve as different stages in similar ecosystems in different locations.

If we study a pond or a small section of a marsh or an open field, we might conclude that it is in a condition of balance. Much of the energy that entered the ecosystem was used in supporting the life activities of every living thing in the community. The energy not so used is locked up in the bodies of plants (producers), first-level consumers (herbivores), second- and higher-level consumers (carnivores). The minerals essential to life were absorbed from water and soil, and they too are locked in the bodies of the living plants and animals. But plants and animals die and while alive they give off the waste products of living.

How does a system deal with the problems of waste materials and accumulating dead bodies and yet appear to be in a condition of balance? There is obviously another important job or niche in all ecosystems. This is the job of sanitation and is filled by the *decomposers*. They break down the dead bodies, as well as the waste materials, and convert them into simpler chemicals that re-enter the environment where they are available for use again. Most of the decomposers are microscopically small. Bacteria, molds, and other fungi are the major factors in recycling essential chemicals in all types of ecosystems.

The details of some mineral cycles and the recycling of water and of the gases oxygen and carbon dioxide will be developed in a later chapter. It is important to note here that energy is not recycled. The sun has unfailingly poured out its radiant energy for billions of years in the past and will probably continue to do so well into the future. This means that each day a new supply of energy pours down on the green plants of the biosphere. The mineral substances of most importance include salts of nitrogen, phosphorus, sulfur, and a few others. These are used in relatively small amounts and their regular recycling insures an available supply at all times.

This is a good time to look at portions of different ecosystems. You will be trying to identify some of the living things in each habitat that fill the important niches of producer, first-level consumer, and second-level consumer. You will also try to recognize the structure within each ecosystem observed.

You may be troubled by the need to identify the specific living things that perform the main jobs in maintaining the structure of the ecosystem. It is not necessary at this point to be precise in your identifications. Plants can be named as herbs, grasses, trees, shrubs, ferns, mosses, etc., while birds, insects, worms, snails, spiders, beetles, ants, larvae, and similar identifications will serve for the animals.

As you proceed with your ecological studies you will probably want to identify the living things you observe more exactly. There will be some materials to help you achieve this aim in later chapters. A second goal is to become familiar with and to use some of the equipment and techniques that are part of the ecologist's bag of tricks.

EXPERIMENT 3. To Observe and Study the Structure of a Pond Community.

Materials and Equipment. Hand lens; kitchen strainer with attached wooden handle; plankton net; white enamel pan, or plastic margarine tubs; plastic bags; jars (both glass and plastic); rubber bands; field notebook; widemouthed gallon jar, or small aquarium; a waterscope.

1. Any pond you choose to observe will have some structure. Each pond will show a number of zones or layers. Not all layers are represented in all ponds, but the diagram shows what you should look for. The zones are recognized by the plants found in them. The plants, as producers, attract the animals that feed on them.

Imagine that you are in a small rowboat in a pond, slowly approaching the shore. You first move through the clear water until you can look down and see some submerged plants rooted in the pond bottom. These include stoneworts, bladderworts, fanworts and waterweeds. As you come closer to the shore you see the floating leaf plants; water lilies and duckweed among others; finally the edge of the pond where there is a zone of plants rooted in the shallow bottom soil with the upper part of the plants sticking out of the water. Here the plants include cattails, pickerelweeds, and arrowheads among others.

After you land and move slowly away from the pond, you pass through a meadow area followed by zones of shrubs, then the small and the large trees of a wood or forest. Not all these areas or zones will necessarily be evident in every pond, and you can try to decide what caused some to be absent in the pond you explore.

In the pond itself, there are three vertical zones in which the animals present will help you. On the surface of the pond, you will recognize insects such as the water striders and whirligig beetles and possibly some small snails whose weight is supported by the surface film of the water. The middle layer is the water below the surface and extends down to a point about 8 inches from the bottom. Here you will see fishes, tadpoles, diving beetles, and countless other smaller animals that graze on the microscopic plants and animals found floating and drifting in the upper waters just below the surface.

The bottom of a pond might be a layer of sand or gravel or mud, depending on its location and the materials that drain into it and settle on the bottom. It is a world of its own design with living things equipped to survive in the special type of habitat it is. It is, of course, part of the pond ecosystem and interacts with it. It is worth exploring alone also.

This is designed as an exploratory experience. It is an opportunity to examine a pond ecosystem and to recognize something of its organization and structure. Mainly you will be trying to identify the major producers and consumers in each part of the pond. This does not mean a precise identification. As you explore natural situations, you will become aware of the more conspicuous plants and animals and will learn how to see the less conspicuous ones. Meeting these living things often will stimulate you to learn their names. The references in Appendix II include a number that can help you to identify many of the organisms accurately. Help is also to be found in many other places such as a local gardener or florist; your biology or science teacher; or museums, zoos, and botanical gardens whose staffs are only too willing to assist.

The pond will call you back for visits many times. There are changes with the seasons, so there is always something to observe. Even a small pond supports many hundreds of varieties of plants and animals. Many of these are quite small and it takes patience and some skill to recognize them. Most can be seen in some detail with a hand lens (Figure 7), a tool you will always carry with you wherever you go. With a hand lens in your pocket you can reach into a world as

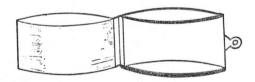

Figure 7. A folding hand lens. This will be your most important tool. The best one for all-round use is a 10X magnifier. In use, you will place the lens very close to your eye.

fascinating and exciting as any the biosphere has to offer. All of these are worth the effort it takes to observe them; each a success in its special environment.

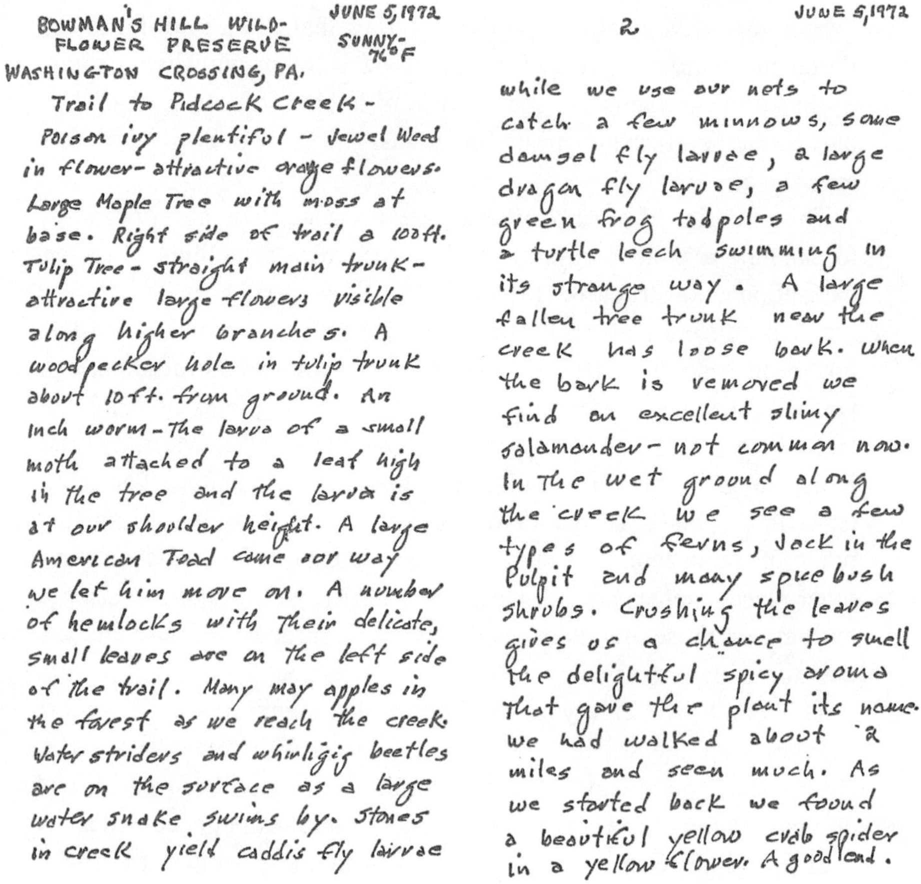

BOWMAN'S HILL WILD-
FLOWER PRESERVE
WASHINGTON CROSSING, PA.

JUNE 5, 1972
SUNNY-
76°F

Trail to Pidcock Creek -
Poison ivy plentiful - Jewel Weed in flower - attractive orange flowers. Large Maple Tree with moss at base. Right side of trail a 100 ft. Tulip Tree - straight main trunk - attractive large flowers visible along higher branches. A woodpecker hole in tulip trunk about 10 ft. from ground. An inch worm - the larva of a small moth attached to a leaf high in the tree and the larva is at our shoulder height. A large American Toad came our way we let him move on. A number of hemlocks with their delicate, small leaves are on the left side of the trail. Many may apples in the forest as we reach the creek. Water striders and whirligig beetles are on the surface as a large water snake swims by. Stones in creek yield caddis fly larvae

2

JUNE 5, 1972

while we use our nets to catch a few minnows, some damsel fly larvae, a large dragon fly larvae, a few green frog tadpoles and a turtle leech swimming in its strange way. A large fallen tree trunk near the creek has loose bark. When the bark is removed we find an excellent slimy salamander - not common now. In the wet ground along the creek we see a few types of ferns, Jack in the Pulpit and many spice bush shrubs. Crushing the leaves gives us a chance to smell the delightful spicy aroma that gave the plant its name. We had walked about 2 miles and seen much. As we started back we found a beautiful yellow crab spider in a yellow flower. A good end.

Figure 8. Two pages of a field notebook with observations from a field trip.

2. Record in your field notebook (Figure 8) the main producers you find growing in the waters at the pond's edge. If you do not know their names, list them as herbs, shrubs, trees, floating plants, rooted plants, and submerged plants. Is any one type more plentiful than the others? Examine leaves and stems for signs of animals or of feeding by animals. What kinds of plant eaters were you able to find? Record all the evidence you gather as you proceed with your exploration.

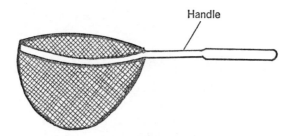

Figure 9. A kitchen-strainer water net. Any size from a diameter of 4 to 6 inches is excellent. A 3- to 6-foot wooden piece can be attached to the strainer with wire, cord, or waterproof tape.

3. Use a fine kitchen strainer (Figure 9) with a long handle to sweep through the shallow water about a foot or two from the edge. Half-fill a white enamel pan with pond water. Transfer the animals and plants collected with the strainer to the pan. Each animal will be outlined against the white bottom of the pan and will be easy to observe. Note and record all the information you gather about the life you find. Continue to sweep the strainer through different sections of the water's edge and add the collection to the enamel pan. If you do not have a pan, you can use a number of plastic margarine tubs which work in the same fashion. How many different types of animals did you collect? Are they plant eaters or animal eaters? Use your hand lens to look closely for any evidence of the way each type feeds.

4. For this investigation, you will need a plankton net. To make a plankton net (Figure 10), you will need a wire coat hanger, a nylon stocking, a small plastic or glass vial, about 20 feet of strong nylon fishing line, ½ inch wide plastic tape, pliers with wire cutter.

a. Cut the question-mark-shaped part of the hanger with the wire cutter and discard it.

b. Push the two wires of the hanger together to form a double strand of wire. Use pliers to bring the two wires close to one another. Now bend the double wire to form a circle which will serve as the frame of the net.

c. Cut a small piece of the stocking at the tip of the toe. This will be the opening for the collecting vial. Insert the vial through the opening so that it projects below the toe. Attach the vial firmly to the

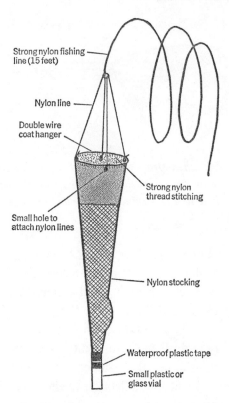

Strong nylon fishing
line (15 feet)

Nylon line

Double wire
coat hanger

Strong nylon
thread stitching

Small hole to
attach nylon lines

Nylon stocking

Waterproof plastic tape

Small plastic or
glass vial

*Figure 10. A plankton net for collecting fresh-water and ma-
rine plankton.*

stocking with plastic tape. Leave the lower part of the vial uncovered
so that you can use your hand lens to see what is collected by the net.

d. Stretch the open end of the stocking over the frame, folding
the top of the stocking over the frame inside the net. Stitch the stocking with strong nylon thread, using close overcast stitches. This will
attach the stocking very firmly to the frame.

e. Make four very small holes in the upper part of the stocking
just below the frame. Attach an 18-inch length of strong nylon fishing line to each hole.

f. Gather the free ends of the four short lines together and tie
them tightly to one another. Then tie one end of a 15-foot length of
nylon cord to the four lines as shown.

g. To use the net, throw it out into the water away from shore
and pull it back toward yourself. The net has such small openings

that the water will escape through them while most of the small living things in the water will be held inside the net. They collect in the vial. A few such sweeps through the water will concentrate all the living things in several gallons of water in the small vial. If you are in a small boat, you can drop the net in the water and drag it for 100 feet or so before bringing in your catch and examining it.

With your plankton net collect water from the pond just below the surface, about 3 or 4 feet from the edge. After you have drawn the net for a distance of 3 or 4 feet, lift it from the water and examine the collecting tube with your hand lens. You should be able to see a number of different tiny plankton plants and animals in the water. Make 6 to 8 sweeps through the water to concentrate the plankton you collect. Does your collection include any producers? Any consumers? How can you easily tell them apart? Do not be concerned about exact identifications here, but do note whether any one or two types are very numerous.

5.   Are there any reducers or decomposers in or near the pond? Look for parts of the bodies of dead plants or animals near or in the water. With your kitchen sieve collect some mud from the pond bottom and transfer it to a fresh enamel pan or margarine tub with pond water. Examine for plants and animals. Would you expect to find reducers here? Why? Record your observations.

6.   Observe the larger animals of the pond as they appear. These could include frogs, toads, salamanders, turtles, snakes, dragonflies, fish, and many others. Locate a spot close to the pond where you can be comfortable and can watch what goes on without moving around and thus disturbing the life around the pond. Try to make yourself part of the pond ecosystem, and your observations will increase as you become absorbed in the life of the community. What activities of each of the animals you saw were you able to observe? Record.

7.   To make a waterscope (Figure 11), you will need a one-foot length of heavy cardboard tubing from 3 to 5 inches in diameter, or a cylindrical container from 6 to 12 inches long from which the two ends can be removed, or a small wooden pail or a small can; $\frac{1}{16}$-inch-thick sheets of plexiglas or regular glass cut to the needed size and shape; Saran Wrap or other heavy transparent plastic; aquarium cement; assorted materials for setting plastic sheets or flexible plastic in place at the bottom of a tube.

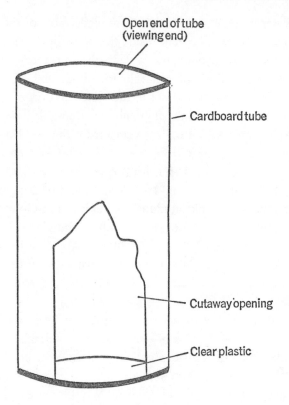

Open end of tube
(viewing end)

Cardboard tube

Cutaway opening

Clear plastic

Figure 11. A waterscope. The closed end of the tube is pushed 2 or 3 inches into the water of a pond, a lake, a tide pool, or similar bodies of water. By looking through the open end of the tube you can see the life of the water below the surface.

The waterscope pictured was improvised from a cardboard container which contained dried parsley. The bottom of the container had clear plastic firmly inserted. We had no difficulty in removing the plastic top of the package. The entire tube was wrapped in plastic tape to waterproof it. It works excellently as a waterscope.

To make a waterscope, if you cannot find a ready-made container with a clear plastic bottom, look for a cardboard tube from which you can get a 6 to 12-inch length. Cover one end with a sheet of Saran Wrap or other flexible plastic sheet. Use rubber bands or string to hold the plastic tightly over the opening. Push the closed end of the tube no more than 2 or 3 inches into the water. Look into the tube at the open end. You will see the life below the surface clearly, without any of the reflections that keep you from seeing effectively any other way. It is as though you were inside the pond and part of it.

Any cylindrical object in which one end is open and the other permits a window opening, which must be covered with a sheet of glass or plastic, can be used to make a waterscope. The big problem is how to insert the glass or plexiglas or other plastic in the window so the water will not push it away or allow water to enter the scope.

A wooden pail might have its bottom inserted in a groove so that a circular piece of glass or plexiglas cut the size of the bottom can replace the wood and be held firmly in place. Some aquarium cement used as a seal around the edges of the glass insert will prevent water from entering the pail. A tin can with both ends removed will serve well if flexible plastic is used as a window, but the inside would have to be painted dull black to remove internal reflections.

8. Use your waterscope to observe underwater activities of animals that live below the surface. This piece of equipment is an effective way of entering the pond environment. It is rather easy to make from simple materials. Note any observations made with the waterscope. What did they add to the other observations you were able to make?

It is possible to bring a small part of the pond ecosystem home and to set it up as a minipond in an aquarium or a widemouthed gallon-size glass jar. This will enable you to observe some of the pond community over a period of months. Your notes will be much more complete and you will have a far more valid picture of the ecosystem and its organization.

EXPERIMENT 4.   Setting Up and Observing a Minipond Ecosystem.

Materials and Equipment. Small aquarium (1- or 2-gallon capacity); gallon-size, widemouthed jars with covers; quart-size peanut butter jars; fresh-water plants from pond or purchased from tropical-fish shops; clear pond water; collections of pond animals made with kitchen-sieve collector.

Prepare aquarium or glass containers by cleaning and washing them thoroughly. Put a small quantity of pond bottom mud on the bottom of the containers to be used. Cover with a 1-inch layer of washed aquarium sand. Insert 2 or 3 sprigs of aquatic plants in the sand. Carefully and slowly add clear pond water until the aquarium is about three-fourths full. Allow the water to settle for 3 or 4 days. The minipond is now ready for use (Figures 12 and 13).

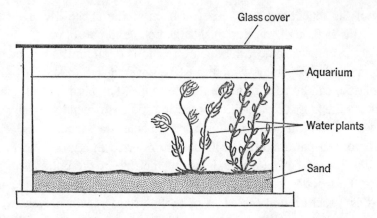

Figure 12. A minipond set up in a commercial-type aquarium.

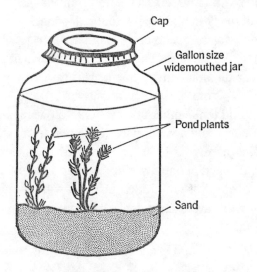

Figure 13. A minipond using a widemouthed gallon jar.

Add some animals from your pond animal collection to the mini-pond. Do not add too many at first. The object is to reach a balance in the ecosystem in which the producers provide enough food for all the life in the pond and the consumers flourish as well. The decomposers break down the wastes and remains while the oxygen and carbon dioxide needed by plants and animals is recycled between them.

Cover the opening of your minipond loosely with glass, cardboard, or the caps of jars. Why? Make sure that the pond is exposed to moderate light? How will you know that there is too much light? If some water is lost by evaporation, replace it. Add or remove some animals if they seem to be decreasing or increasing in numbers. Most of all, observe your pond several times daily and note any events and activities that you feel are worth noting.

Snails will lay eggs on the glass surfaces or on plants in the water. Insect larvae and tadpoles will thrive, and you should be able to maintain the minipond for weeks or even months. You might find it more helpful to set up a few small aquaria than a single large one. Then you can select the specific pond animals you put in each one and can try to establish a balance in each.

In later chapters you will be able to use the small balanced miniponds for performing experiments in which you determine the effects of altering physical conditions such as pH, intensity of light, temperature, and others on the ecosystem. This was just a first look at the pond ecosystem to enable you to become familiar with its broader structure and activities.

EXPERIMENT 5. An Introduction to a Woods' Ecosystem (Spring, Summer, and Fall).

The pond you explored could have been located in a wooded area. If so, it is easy to move on to an exploration of the woods in an effort to identify its structure. If not, it should not be difficult to find a wooded area you can use for the same purpose. For this introductory look you will need only your hand lens and your field notebook. This is an opportunity, also, to sharpen your powers of observation and to see much of what you know is present, especially the animals, which are in hiding or on the move.

Since the producers are rooted in the ground and are always in place, it is best to begin with them. The first feature of the structure of the wood to look for is its vertical arrangement. The ground layer includes small herbaceous plants, mosses, ferns, young trees, and shrubs. These are the producers and they attract plant-eating animals which you may be able to see.

Much of the ground layer contains dead leaves, branches, and other debris. The leaf litter is itself a habitat for many small consumers and decomposers which you can study in some detail in some later investigations. Here and there in a well-established wood you will find fallen trees and parts of trunks in one stage or another of decay. If the bark on a fallen log is loose, lift it away and note the activity within. There will be dozens of animals busily feeding in the protected environment provided by the log. Are you surprised at the kinds of animals you find there? The log community is a special kind of miniecosystem that exists for a short time until the material of the log becomes part of the soil. It, too, is worth remembering as a source of some future investigations. Replace the bark so that the animals within can continue to perform their roles. If the log is light enough to roll over, you might find some other animals living below it. After making your observations and recording them, be sure to return the log to its original position.

How much light reaches these ground-level communities? What factors control the amount of light that penetrates to the surface? What happens to this layer in winter and early spring before the leaves of trees and shrubs appear? When is producer activity greatest in the ground level?

The next layer is the shrub layer. These are woody plants that grow to heights of 3–10 feet. Shrubs are rooted in the spaces between the larger trees. How many different kinds of shrubs do you find? Are there any kinds of trees under which few, if any, shrubs grow? What activities of the trees keep the shrubs out?

The next layer consists of the trees whose height can vary from ten feet to a hundred feet or more. Trees give a feeling of strength and stability and many do manage to live a hundred years or more. The wood ecosystem is dominated by its trees. How many different types of trees can you find? Are any varieties more numerous than others? How far apart are the larger trees? What kinds of plants grow in the spaces between trees? Are any of the trees or shrubs in flower? Have any produced seeds or fruits?

Are any animals feeding on the plants of the wood? Look for signs that leaves, stems, and other plant parts have been used as food. Are any growths visible on stems, leaves, and any other plant structures? What do they tell you? Have you seen any insects flying about, crawling about, or feeding? Are spiders evident? Any signs of frogs or salamanders or snails and slugs? Record in your field notebook any observations you have been able to make. Look for signs in the form of tracks, tooth marks, scratches, and other effects that say to you, an animal was here.

If you are interested in identifying plants and animals you have seen, the references in Appendix II include several that will be very helpful in tracking them down. Since wooded areas are fairly stable, you can return to them again and again to note changes and to fill in details about the structure of an important ecosystem. Also there are changes in the players, the plants, and animals of the woods, as the seasons change.

EXPERIMENT 6. Exploring a Meadow, a Field, or a Vacant Lot (Spring Through Fall).

Meadows, fields, and vacant lots are habitats with plant communities in which there are few woody plants and in which grasses, herbs, and similar non-woody plants predominate. This determines the kinds of animals these producers support. A vacant lot is not a true ecosystem, but it is an interesting opportunity to observe the colonization of a piece of city or town land by plants and then animals, to form a temporary community of living things. When a field or a meadow is not easy to reach, the vacant lot will make it possible to observe plants and animals that have succeeded in surviving in a difficult environment.

Your aim in making any of these explorations is to examine associations of plants and animals and the chain of relationships that produce the community of which they are a part. Look for major plants in terms of their numbers and for the herbivores and carnivores they support. Make records of your observations since only accurate recorded notes are effective in ecological work. You may also want to note questions that occur to you and any thoughts about later visits you want to make to the same area, to follow up some process you have observed.

These explorations were included here to enable you to become familiar with the joy and challenges of field studies and investigations. At the same time, you become aware of the similar basic structure of all living communities and the close ties that relate organisms to one another. Everything in the biosphere is related to everything else.

4 | Investigating Life on Land

LIFE ON LAND. When living things moved out of the sea onto the land, they were there to stay. They flourished, and over the years they succeeded in occupying every land area that could support life. The living things able to adapt to the conditions of life were the ones that survived. Adapting means adjusting, and the living things you observe as you explore the communities in land habitats are their success stories.

You can observe the structure, behavior, and aspects of the life histories of individual living things to try to learn how they contribute to success. How does it help the monarch butterfly to lay its eggs on milkweed leaves? Do any other insects lay eggs on the milkweed plant? What would happen if there were two varieties of butterfly eggs on the milkweed and the caterpillars of both types emerged at the same time?

You might, instead, look at the entire ecosystem of any one of a number of possible types of land habitats to try to recognize the broad interrelationships among the different living things in the community. There are so many types of land habitats with their contained communities that there will be no problem in finding challenges to your investigative talents.

Each habitat supports its community with its variety of populations of living things. The populations are interrelated in food chains and food webs, each in a kind of balance. There is also a flexibility in the balance and changes do occur. Each community is unique, yet it shares a common basic structure with other communities. It is this characteristic that makes each place you visit a situation full of challenges to which you will want to respond.

The problem of finding land habitats for investigation is not at all difficult. Why not begin right at home and make an inventory of available situations? First there are the grounds around our own homes— back or front yards or both. They may not look promising to you but how carefully have you looked before? You can observe frequently over a period of time and will find that there is an interesting ecological story to unfold. Most yards are small enough to be explored in their entirety.

A yard may be mostly lawn with the edges planted with cultivated flowers and shrubs. It might include a vegetable garden and a few fruit or ornamental trees. Some may be neglected or even abused, but there will be many plants which have rootholds in the soil and they survive. Seeds of plants from adjoining yards and even from greater distances find their way to some bit of soil where they can get the water and sunlight they need to take hold.

There will always be some kinds of animals that feed on plants— usually insects. But there is also a quota of earthworms, pill bugs, and other small creatures. Birds and other insect eaters will regularly visit the yard and will find what they need there. By observing regularly, you will build up an inventory of plants and animals as well as of some relationships between them that illustrate some ecological ideas. This place might be the area to begin to learn the names of some of the more common plants and animals you meet. You might also begin to look into the life histories of some of the more interesting ones.

EXPERIMENT 7. Observation and Study of an Abandoned Yard.

A yard which is no longer cared for and cultivated presents an opportunity to observe some interesting processes. Draw a rough sketch of the yard (Figure 14) and note the plants which are most numerous. Are they plants that had been planted there which managed to survive? If the yard once had a lawn, have any plants replaced some of the grasses? Are any animals visible? What kinds? Are they associated with any particular plants?

What plants have invaded the open-soil areas? You might want to number each of the plant types for recording them on your sketch map. Take one of each type for later identification. Use references in the appendix to help you in identifying the plants you collect.

What kind of soil is in the yard? What is its color? Is its texture sand, gravel, clay, or humus? Is there much water available in the

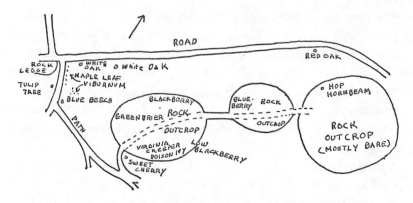

Figure 14. A sketch map of a park area most of whose plants are native to the area with a few introduced types.

soil? Try to pour a pint or two of water onto a small section of soil (12×12 inches) and note how long it takes to be absorbed. Is every part of the yard exposed to direct sunlight for an hour or more every day? Is there any relation between exposure to light and the amount of plant growth?

What animals are visible? What are they doing? Are there any woody plants standing in the yard? Note their location on the sketch map. How much small-plant growth is there under the trees? How can you explain what you find? Look in the crevices of the bark and along branches and on leaves for small animals. Are any of them feeding on the tree? Is there any sign of eggs laid by insects? Collect the eggs you find and keep them in small covered containers in which you keep a small piece of moist paper toweling. Moisten the toweling regularly and observe the changes that occur daily.

Another convenient area for field explorations is the school grounds. This is true even though the unpaved surface is small. Some kinds of plants will manage to establish themselves in the exposed soil. Plant-eating animals are sure to follow. Since all open areas in towns and cities are likely to be disturbed by man's activities, long-term relationships are not likely to be seen. It will be possible to investigate those plants, especially, which are able to survive because in some way or ways they are adapted to flourish in environments that are not quite ideal.

EXPERIMENT 8. A Study of Some Food Chains in a Schoolyard.

During the school year you spend some time daily in the schoolyard. You have a chance to observe regularly and over a long period of time. Many schools have gardens and are often bordered by hedges or bushes. There should be a variety of plants even in a small area. These will attract a variety of consumers. There will be a number of types of insects, slugs, land snails, spiders, and others.

Record all observation of feeding. Note the feeder and the plant that is eaten. Are any birds present? Do they feed on insects or are they seedeaters? Are any of the animals laying eggs?

The soil has its populations of animals. Some of these are found on or near the surface or under small stones, twigs and boards. Earthworms are especially common after a heavy rain. Can you explain why? You will also see centipedes, millipedes, pill bugs, and others. What do these animals use as food? What is their niche (job) in the community?

What are the main kinds of plants? Is any one type more plentiful than the others? If there is, how can you tell what makes it successful? Remove a single plant carefully from the soil. What kinds of roots does it have? How could they contribute to the plant's success? Is the plant in flower? Do you see any seeds? How many seeds does the plant produce? If flowers and seeds are not seen, keep watching the plant until they do appear.

Some of your observations may lead you to ask questions about relationships other than in food chains. You may feel that you want to explore the other relationships more fully. How do you interpret these observations? Was what you saw unexpected? How would you go about finding answers to your questions?

Vacant lots, bits of land on which no buildings stand or which are not being cultivated, make excellent areas for study. If you are fortunate and locate one which has recently been cleared, you have an opportunity to observe the way in which it will be colonized by plants.

Any section of cleared land whose surface shows no plant growth can be used to observe the invasion by plants whose seeds are carried to the open soil by wind, water, or by animals. The type of soil and other conditions will determine which plants manage to take root and to thrive.

EXPERIMENT 9.   To Observe the Colonization of a Small Section of Bare Soil.

Materials and Equipment.   Four small wooden stakes; hand lens; 12-inch-square quadrat; field notebook.

This investigation is best begun in early spring. Mark off with the stakes the boundaries of your plot—about 10 feet square. Select a section of open soil in the middle of a larger bare area. Why?

Make your observations at weekly intervals at first. Look for seeds that land on the soil and for any young plants that begin to show aboveground. Draw a square on a large sheet of paper and record the spot where you find evidence of the arrival of plants.

Continue your weekly observations as more and more plants appear. Are they all of the same type? Can you recognize any of them? Look at the nearest area to your plot in which plants are growing. Do any of your seedlings (young plants) resemble plants growing in the adjacent plot? Did you expect this result? Why?

By late spring or early summer, there should be a sizable number of plants. Can you estimate the total number of plants growing in the

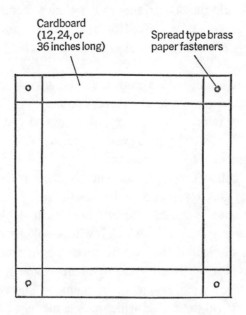

Figure 15. A quadrat used for selecting areas for sampling. This is a major tool of plant ecologists.

entire plot? Drop a 12-inch-square cardboard quadrat (Figure 15) at random in a part of the larger plot.

To make a quadrat you need four lengths of heavy cardboard 2 inches wide and either 12 inches, 24 inches, and 36 inches long. You can assemble the three different size quadrats by attaching them in the form of a square with large brass spread-type paper fasteners. If you prefer to make the quadrats of wood, use four lengths of each of the previously described dimensions of wood strips. Drill small holes at both ends of each strip and fasten with small bolts with fitting nuts.

Count the number of plants within the quadrat. How many different types of plants are there within the quadrat?

You will recognize this count as a sample. How could you estimate the total number of plants in the entire plot? Are you satisfied with your estimate? Drop your quadrat in another section of the experimental plot. Count the total number of plants in the quadrat and the number of different types. Estimate from the second sample the total plot count. How does it compare with the first estimate?

If the area is not disturbed, continue your observations until the fall. What changes in plant populations occur? Do any new plant types appear in large numbers? Are any of the original plant types reduced in numbers? What happened to them? Were they crowded out by other plants? Did they grow rapidly and then produce their flowers and seeds? Was there too much rain, or not enough? Were there any other causes of the results you obtained?

The ideal study would continue the observations through another year or two. In time more and more new plant types would reach the plot and the changes in the plant populations would be evident. There would be other changes as the consumer populations followed their food sources. These changes and the relationships between producers and consumers would provide another investigation worth some attention.

Parks, nature preserves, museums, and conservation centers are found in all parts of the country. They provide a wide variety of land habitats which are not available for your own investigations, but they frequently have one or more nature trails with identification of major plant types. There are also well-marked-out ecological processes for your observation.

These are the facilities in which you can observe and add to the plants you can recognize. They will make much of your later work more meaningful and productive. Here, too, you can find expert help in interpreting your own investigations.

Since collecting is prohibited in most such areas, these are the places in which to practice sketching and photography as used in ecological studies. Often there will also be exhibits of the larger animals of the area in small zoos and aquaria. The staffs of these institutions are also available for help in identification of animals and plants you find in your own studies.

Fields and meadows are to be found outside the larger cities. Visiting one is a rewarding experience. Here you will find attractive communities with many ecological relationships waiting to be observed and unraveled.

The sun shines bright over field and meadow since there are few trees and shrubs to shade the smaller plants. The dominant plants are called herbs or herbaceous plants. This means that they do not have the woody tissues found in trees and shrubs. Many of the plants of field and meadow have short life spans, so there are seasonal changes in the conspicuous plants of these land habitats.

The animals found in field and meadow are not the same as those found in other land ecosystems. There are many types of insects that fill a range of niches and they attract a variety of larger consumers that feed on them. Changes of longer duration occur slowly as woody plants begin to appear and prosper. They affect the plants that flourish in bright sunshine as the ground beneath the trees is shaded by the canopy of leaves. Ultimately a wooded or forest area replaces the field or meadow, if man does not interfere when he cuts down the woody plants, and in other ways disturbs the developing ecosystem.

The soils of some fields and meadows associated with streams are wet, and they will support different kinds of plants than will a field in which the soil is generally dry. The specific types of animals in the two kinds of environment will be determined by the kinds of plants found in them.

EXPERIMENT 10.   To Survey a Field or Meadow in the Spring and Early Summer for Its Plant Populations.

Materials and Equipment.   Field notebook; hand lens; a 24×24-inch quadrat; plastic bags with ties; small collecting bottles and vials with covers or screw caps; pooter for collecting small insects; small amount of rubbing alcohol.

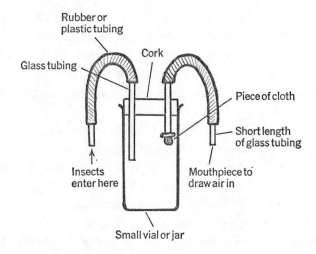

Figure 16. A pooter for collecting small insects by using re-duced air pressure.

To make a pooter (Figure 16), you need a small vial or jar, a 2-hole rubber or cork stopper, four pieces of glass tubing—two pieces 3 inches long and two pieces 1½ inches long—two lengths of rubber or plastic 6 inches long, a small piece of muslin or other cloth.

Insert the two 3-inch lengths of glass tubing in the openings of a 2-hole stopper. Cover the inside end of one tube with a small piece of muslin or other porous cloth tied tightly to the tube.

Insert the stopper in the jar or vial and add a length of rubber or plastic tubing to the glass tubes in the stopper. Now insert the smaller lengths of glass tubing in the free ends of the rubber tubing.

To use, draw the air through the tube connected to the muslin-covered end in the jar. This will draw the air into the jar through the other tube. Hold the end of the intake tube close to an insect and it will be drawn into the jar. The pooter can also be used to collect small aquatic animals from tide pools and from small fresh-water pools.

Begin in the spring by surveying the field for its important larger plants. Note the trees and shrubs and record their numbers. Use one of the references to identify the plants.

Use the 2-foot-square quadrat to sample the herbaceous plants in two separate quadrats. Record the five most numerous plants and the number of each type in each of the sample collections. Record in your notebook. Try to identify the important ones.

Note for each of the plant types whether it is in flower or has already produced seeds. Indicate also the approximate size of each type.

Were your sample plots good representations of the whole plot? Were the types and numbers of the most numerous plants the same in each sample? Do you think your results would be more accurate if you added a few more random samples?

If you see animals as you explore the area collect them or note them in the field notebook for use in the next investigation.

When you return to your plot in the fall, you will find the same trees and shrubs as you noted in the spring. Use the 2-foot-square quadrat (or more samples if you think it necessary) to select random samples of the herbaceous plants and grasses. Note the five most numerous types and record along with the numbers of each type.

Were there differences in the types of herbs in the spring and in the fall? Were the plants in comparable stages of development? Did any types live from spring through the summer into the fall?

EXPERIMENT 11.   To Survey and Inventory the Types of Animals Supported by the Plants of Field and Meadow.

Fields and meadows are rich in plants which produce enough food to support many populations of animals. Look first for evidences of the activities of animals that feed on plants. Some, such as caterpillars, grasshoppers, land snails, slugs, beetles, mice, rabbits, and deer feed on leaves, buds, and young stems. Record any animals you observe feeding or such evidence as partly eaten leaves and other plant parts.

Other vegetarians suck plant juices. These include plant lice (aphids) and bugs which feed on plant sap, while butterflies, moths, bees, and flies feed on nectar in the flowers. Record all your observations of this feeding method including the plant used as food and the animal feeding on it.

A number of animals feed on fruit or seeds of plants. These include weevils, caterpillars, mice, squirrels, and birds. These require close looking. Record all your observations.

Some insects lay their eggs inside the leaves, buds, or stems of a number of plants. The plant reacts by enlarging its tissues around the egg and forming a structure called a *gall*. Each gall structure is characteristic of the plant and insect combination. Gall insects each use a specific plant for egg laying and the plant responds by producing the same enlarged structure. The egg gives rise to a larva which feeds on the plant matter in the gall and completes its development into an adult insect after going through a quiet period called the pupal stage. The adult insect, mostly small wasps, emerge from the gall and lay their eggs in a new generation of plants. Goldenrods and milkweeds often have galls, mainly on their stems. Cut open a few galls with a knife and look for the egg, larva, or pupa within. Most gall formers are woody plants. Oaks, hickories, maples, blueberries, blackberries, and other woody plants each support many types of galls.

Other animals feed on bark (bark beetles, wood lice, and millipedes) or they bore through wood (wood wasp, beetle larvae) or they feed on roots (moth larvae, beetle larvae). Look for evidences of each of these and record your results.

Wherever there are plants and plant eaters you will also find animal eaters (carnivores). They include ladybirds and other beetles, spiders, centipedes, praying mantises, and others. Look for evidences of carnivores in action.

Waste feeders (scavengers) are also present. They include earthworms, slugs, pill and sow bugs, fly larvae, and some beetles.

Was there a difference in the types of animals you found active in the spring and in the fall? How would you explain the difference or the absence of a difference?

Hardwood forests and woods once covered much of the land area of the United States. Even though they are now reduced in numbers, it is still possible to find good hardwood forests for exploration. Woody plants are the giants of the plant world. They include trees, shrubs, and vines. But it is the trees that dominate the forest and are involved in the lives of all the animals and the smaller plants found there. The world of trees is a vast one and forests and woods of some kind are to be found in most sections of America.

Nearly a thousand different varieties of trees and shrubs are found today in the United States. But a relatively small number of types of trees can be used to observe and study the ecology of wooded areas. Forests are described in terms of the dominant tree types in them. Thus there are oak-hickory forests, hemlock forests, white pine forests, Douglas fir forests, and beech-maple forests among others.

A forest and its many trees is a place where animals of many varieties can find shelter, food, and a place to breed. It also provides the conditions favorable for enormous numbers of smaller, herbaceous plants to flourish.

There are two main types of forest trees. The pines, spruces, firs, cedars, and similar plants make up the softwood forests. These trees have small needlelike or scalelike leaves and they produce their seeds in cones. Most of them keep some of their leaves throughout the year (evergreens). The ancestors of the modern evergreens were the earliest of the trees to appear on the earth.

Maples, oaks, hickories, birches, and countless other hardwoods lose their broad, flat leaves seasonally, and they bear flowers in which the seeds are produced. Their dominant varieties live in associations with other trees, as well as with shrubs, vines, herbs, mosses, and ferns.

Forests make many contributions to the stability of areas far beyond their borders. The trees and the forest floor serve as huge sponges which hold tremendous amounts of water. The water passes through the trees and other plants slowly, as it serves its purposes in the functioning of the plants. Surplus water is evaporated slowly from the leaves into the air to form clouds and to function in the water cycle.

Forests have an interesting layered structure. The branches of the larger dominant trees, when covered with leaves, capture much of the sunlight falling on them. Smaller amounts of sunlight filter through the network of branches to reach the lower layers of a forest. The plants in the lower layers are adapted to function best in lower levels of light.

Below the canopy of the upper branches, many birds, squirrels, and large numbers of insects are active. The shrubs and shorter trees form a second layer with its own populations of animals. The herbaceous plants including flowering plants and ferns, as well as the mosses and many fungi, occupy the floor layer with its resident-animal populations. Many parts of the floor are occupied by leaf litter, fallen branches, and the trunks of dead trees whose decomposition returns materials to the soil. Finally, the soil itself supports an unusual group of animal populations, as well as many microbes.

There are dozens of interesting and productive investigations, explorations, and studies you can make in a hardwood forest. Three or four will be outlined in detail below. A number of others will be suggested in sufficient detail to enable you to design your own experimental plan.

EXPERIMENT 12.   A Study of Life in a Hardwood Forest.

Materials and Equipment.   Hand lens; field notebook; plastic bags with ties; screw-cap jars and vials; 2-foot-square quadrat; tape measure; white cloth beating tray; photographic light meter (if available); pooter for small insects; bird glasses (if available); 8×10 sheets of graph paper.

The object of this investigation is to examine the community of a hardwood forest (oak-hickory or maple or maple-birch, etc.). One visit a week to gather data should be enough to observe a number of interrelationships. It is not necessary to identify more than the important (in numbers) plants and animals in the community.

Select a typical area in the forest about 50×50 feet. This will serve as a large quadrat. Use the graph paper as a map (as in Figure 17), with the smaller squares as places to record the important plants found. You will be looking for trees, shrubs, and herbs at first.

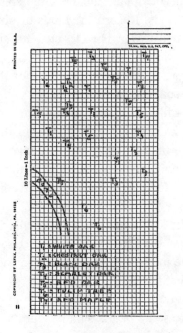

Figure 17.   A graph-paper map of an area known as the Five Oaks Hill. Five different species of oak are the dominant plants of the habitat.

Look for the dominant trees of the quadrat. These may form the canopy of that part of the forest. Look skyward to get the feeling of what a canopy is. Measure the circumference of each large tree with a tape measure and estimate its height. Record the tree's location on the map; use T_1 as a symbol for the dominant tree variety. Make a count of the number of T_1 you can find in the 50×50-foot area. Locate each with its symbol on the map.

As you move through the quadrat, decide whether there is another variety of large tree that is a subdominant—fewer in number than the dominant. Use the symbol T_2 and locate each on the map. In your field notebook include data on circumference and height.

Measure the light intensity at ground level with a photo light meter at four different locations under four different T_1 trees. Record the readings in your notebook and on the map.

Make a list of the shrubs found at the places you made your light readings. These can serve as samples for the entire plot. Use the symbols S_1, S_2, etc., to put them on the map.

Observe the herbaceous plants in the same stations in which light measurements were made. Record the kinds of plants and their numbers. Use symbols such as H_1, H_2, H_3, etc., for these. Use reference works in making your identifications.

If the light readings were different for any of the stations, did you find different herbaceous plants growing?

Animals are generally active and they move around from place to place. The larger animals move through greater distances and are not easy to observe since they are alert to any danger and are easily startled into moving away. You may see signs of their presence by droppings, hoofprints and footprints, and signs of feeding on the bark and leaves of young trees.

Concentrate on the smaller animals, especially insects. You will be able to watch them in the process of feeding. Use your hand lens for close-up views of the method of feeding and the adaptations of different insects for food getting.

When you have recorded your observations in your notebook, you may want to capture some of the smaller ones with the pooter. This device is easy to use and it will enable you to get a closer look at some of the insects.

Another method of getting insects is to make an improvised beating tray (a three-foot square of white or light cloth) which is placed on the ground below some shrubs or small trees. Strike the branches above the cloth a sharp blow with a stick. Most small animals will be dislodged and fall onto the cloth. They can be captured there and examined. Put some in small vials for closer examination.

The mosses, lichens, and ferns, along with leaf litter and soil, are parts of the forest community and each offers opportunities for in-dividual investigations. Some of these will be included in chapter 7.

EXPERIMENT 13.   To Study an Individual Oak, or Maple, or Other coat hanger, pliers with a wire cutter.
Mature Hardwood Tree.

Materials and Equipment.   Hand lens; field notebook; tape measure; pooter; 4×4-inch quadrat; plastic bags and ties; vials and jars with screw caps; a beating tray.

To make a 4×4-inch quadrat (Figure 18) you will need a wire

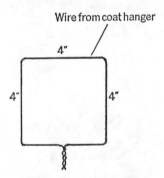

Figure 18.   A 4×4-inch wire quadrat for sampling small areas for mosses, lichens, and other small plants.

Remove the hanger portion of the coat hanger with the wire cutter. Straighten out the long piece of wire of which the hanger is made. Cut off a 20-inch length of wire and use it to make the quadrat. Bend the wire in the middle to make a right angle with two 10-inch arms. Measure 4 inches from the bend on each arm. Make a right-angle bend at the 4-inch mark in each arm, bending both toward the middle. Six inches remain in each arm. If each is bent in a right angle at the 4-inch mark, the 4-inch square is complete with 2 inches extra in each arm which can be twisted into a handle.

The object of this investigation is to observe and study the structure and life history of a single tree and to note and record the major events in its activities through a one-year period. It will also include an investigation of the animals and plants that live in association with the tree.

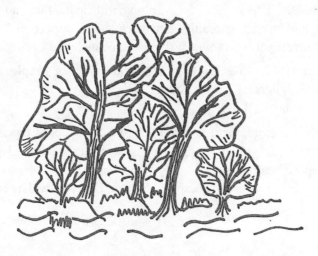

Figure 19.   A group of white oaks.

Figure 20.   White oak leaf and acorn.

Select a mature oak or maple tree. Try to find one that is more or less isolated from other large trees. Is it fully exposed to sun, wind, and rain? Note its position in your field notebook. Include the positions of the nearest large trees. Note also what herbaceous plants grow in its shade.

Measure the circumference of the trunk about five feet above the ground. Estimate the tree's height. Measure the spread of its longest branches. How old do you estimate the tree to be? Remember that if you have chosen an oak tree that the oak is a slow-growing tree.

Start your observations in the spring and continue them at weekly intervals. Note the dates when the leaves first appear, when the flowers appear, when acorns are seen and when the leaves drop in the fall. Collect acorns in the fall and store them in a box with some leaf litter. Store the box in a cold place over the winter. Plant a number of acorns in the forest where there is some open space. Keep a record of the plantings and watch for the young oaks to emerge. What percentage of the acorns planted produced new trees?

Collect a number (25–30) of fully developed leaves. Arrange them in the order of their length. Measure the length of the shortest and the longest leaves and record. Measure the width of the same two leaves. How much variation is there in the length and width?

Figure 21. Bracket fungus on an oak trunk.

Look for bracket fungi or any other signs of parasites attached to or growing on the tree. Note their position and describe them in your field notebook. Inspect the bark for greenish, grayish-green, or gray flat structures. The green ones are likely to be algae, microscopic green plants more usually found in water. The others are lichens, unusual plants that are a partnership of an alga with a fungus. Each of the partners contributes to the success of the pair.

Look at each visit for the insects and other small animals associated with the tree. Record all that you observe. Collect eggs, larvae, and other stages of the life history. Use a larval cage (Figure 22) to follow the life cycle at home. Examine the crevices of the bark for the small animals to be found there. Collect with a pooter. Use the beating tray to collect others.

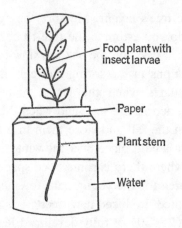

Figure 22. A larval feeding cage. The lower jar contains water and is covered with a sheet of paper with an opening for the stem of a plant that projects into the inverted jar. The leaves are kept fresh for the larvae which feed on them. Change the plant when fresh leaves are needed.

What birds and fur-bearing animals are associated with the tree? Note when you observed feeding and nest-building activities.

Are any mosses growing at the base of the trunk or in the soil close to the trunk? Use the 4×4-inch quadrat to mark off a section of mosses. Use your hand lens to study the detailed structure of the mosses. How many different varieties seem to be growing in the quadrat? Look for young oak seedlings close to the base. What shrubs are able to grow in the shade of the oak?

Look over leaves and stems for galls. The oak is a favorite host for the young of many gall-forming insects. Note all that you find. Collect a number of them and take them home to put them in a vivarium to observe the emergence of the adult insect.

The needle-leaved evergreen trees are the dominant trees of the softwood forests. Pines, firs, spruces, hemlocks, cedars, and others are the best known of these trees. In many parts of the United States there are extensive forests of evergreens. Some of the forests include some hardwoods such as maples, oaks, or others. When there are a sizable number of hardwoods growing together with the softwoods, the forest is called a mixed forest. You should be able to reach a good-sized stand of softwoods for investigation.

When you walk into a pine forest, you are struck by how dark it is and how quiet. The canopy formed by the tall, straight trees keeps most light from reaching the ground. With little light you expect to find few plants providing ground cover. The floor of the forest is covered with fallen pine needles that form a soft carpet. And the fragrance is so invigorating that you will long remember it.

The fallen needles contain resins which are slowly leached out of the needles and enter the soil. The low level of light along with the resins make the soil unfit to support most ground plants. Notice how high the lowest branches are on the trunk of the larger trees. The older branches are the ones nearer the ground. As the tree grows and gives off new branch growth, the younger branches shut off the light which does not reach the lower ones. The lower branches die and they drop from the tree. You can see the sites of the fallen older branches of the tree on the trunk.

The story of other softwood forests is similar with differences in detail. There are references in Appendix II that will help you to identify the more important living types of this type of forest ecosystem.

EXPERIMENT 14.   To Investigate a Softwood (Pine) Forest.

Materials and Equipment.   Hand lens; field notebook; pooter; plastic bags and ties; 4×4 inch wire quadrat; photo light meter.

Since you can walk freely through a pine forest, you can observe it by following a straight-line path for a hundred or two hundred feet. As you proceed slowly, look right and left for any signs of animal life —especially the smaller animals.

Take light-level readings with the light meter in 3 or 4 locations. Is there any variation in the readings? How do the light levels compare with those you made in the hardwood forest? Why?

Search the woods for fungi. There are two main types: the fleshy mushrooms that emerge from the soil, and the woody, or fleshy, bracket fungi found attached to the trunks of standing trees and fallen logs. Check with references for the types you find. Make sketches if it will help you recall their appearance.

Use the procedures from Experiment 1A to measure the pH of the soil from 2 or 3 different sites with hydrion paper. Record and compare with the reading for the hardwood forest.

Lichens of many types are common in softwood forests. Sometimes they are flat, circular, pale green, gray, and sometimes other-colored masses growing on the trunks of trees. Others are found near the bases of the trees as formed bodies bearing such names as pixie cups, British soldiers, and red caps. Use the 4×4-inch wire quadrat to sample the lichens growing on the trunks of 20 different trees and the ones growing on the ground near the trees. Record your results.

Look for insects on the trunk and on the ground. Collect all you can with a pooter and record the results in your notebook. Look also for signs of activity of larger animals. What birds do you see or hear?

Where would you look for young pine seedlings? Why would you expect to find them there? Collect cones from the ground and shake the seeds from them onto a sheet of paper. Plant groups of the seeds in a milk-carton planter using soil from the pine forest. How many of the seeds yielded young plants?

5 | Life in
and Around Water

Oceans, seas, and bays and the land areas in contact with them make up the salt-water habitats in which marine communities flourish. The seashore is the region between the land and the sea that is affected by tides. It is richly colonized by a variety of living things. Since the shore area is the part of marine habitats most available for exploration, most attention will be given to it. If you do not live fairly close to one of the coasts, you might not be able to make the many visits required for a thorough study.

The character of the shore varies widely from one place to another. The land may slope gradually toward the water or the drop may be very steep. The surface of the shore may consist of rocks, pebbles, flat large stones (shingle beaches), clay or mud or a combination of a few of these. Each type supports its own type of populations of living things. And each has its own type of problems for the living things found in it.

Rocky shores are affected by strong wave action. Attaching animals and plants are common here. Barnacles, brown seaweeds, anemones, and the shelled snails and limpets. Sandy and muddy shores favor those animals that can burrow quickly below the surface. The animals able to dig below the surface include many worms, starfishes, clams, and crabs.

Most of the waters of ocean, bay, and sea lie beyond the coast. The inhabitants of most of the marine waters are not affected by tides and they enjoy the advantages of living completely submerged in water. Here there is no weather and the temperature range is small. Light does reach depths of up to 100 feet so the plants in the upper waters, mostly microscopic in size, can perform the life-supporting process of photosynthesis.

It is an advantage to living things to be completely submerged. They do not have to adjust to the wide changes in temperature that affect living things on land. There are no such forces as winds and the other weather factors that also present problems to life on land. The bodies of animals and plants in the ocean are supported in part by the buoyancy of salt waters, and the effects of gravity on them is reduced. Small wonder then that the largest animals ever to live on the earth, the giant whales, live in water. Some of these reach weights of 150 tons (over 300,000 pounds) and it is hard to imagine animals so vast moving about on land.

Life in water is surrounded by this most essential of chemicals. There is no threat of drying out or the consequences that follow for animals and plants that live out their lives away from the shore.

The plants of marine waters produce food in tremendous amounts and they give off comparable amounts of the gas, oxygen. Animals are thus supplied with the oxygen they require for respiration—the process which releases energy stored in food they eat. The waves and other movements of the surface waters dissolve oxygen from the atmosphere when it is required, but marine plants produce vast surpluses of oxygen, much of which reaches the atmosphere.

Those marine plants and animals that live in the intertidal zone, that is, the regions that are submerged and then uncovered as the tides move in and out regularly, face many problems their relatives in the deeper waters do not meet.

They must be equipped to resist the dangers of drying out. Many have hard outer shells or thick, tough body coverings which help keep the body's fluids from evaporating. In beach areas, many animals can dig themselves into the sand or mud and continue to be surrounded by a film of water. Many smaller animals remain hidden and protected in attached seaweeds, in rock crevices, or in cavities in the rocks which remain filled with water between the tides.

The action of waves on beaches and rocky shores batters the living things which they strike. Many of these creatures are equipped to withstand the wave force with heavy outer shells. They are also equipped with effective holdfast structures which anchor them to their support so firmly that they resist injury or being knocked loose.

The attached animals, such as barnacles, and the slow moving ones, such as clams, have interesting and effective ways of getting food. Barnacles are filter feeders, and their limbs keep a stream of water laden with tiny plants and animals, as well as particles of organic matter, moving into the opening of the digestive cavity. Clams are equipped with a pumping system by means of which water carrying food is driven past the mouth opening. The movement of water also reaches large gill systems which extract oxygen from the water flowing over them.

Marine waters do not provide as many varied habitats as does the land, but there are enough opportunities to observe a good many, if you live close enough to the seashore to reach it without too many problems. These are largely the habitats associated with the areas where land and sea meet.

The intertidal areas of rocky shores are especially rich in habitats. Here you can observe and study rock pools and tide pools; crevices and associations of seaweeds; as well as the mud or sandy beach areas which might be quite small.

In addition there are the broad, level, sandy and rocky beaches where another type of habitat can be explored. The tides and waves regularly bring to the shore evidences of sea life from the deeper waters and deposit them for the alert looker to examine.

Estuaries and salt marshes are special habitats which have a particularly important story to tell. Estuaries are formed where rivers and streams run into the sea. Usually the flowing fresh waters follow a riverbed which carries the water into the sea or ocean. At times of tides, the salt waters move up the river valley, sometimes for many miles.

Life in estuaries faces an unusual problem. As salt and fresh waters mix, the salinity of these waters changes. Upstream a river is only slightly salty (brackish), while close to its contact with the sea it is as salty as the ocean itself. Most fresh-water animals and plants cannot tolerate salt while the marine organisms are largely intolerant to fresh water. Some animals and plants are able to live in both types of water without damage.

Rivers and streams carry considerable loads of silt, sand, and other soil particles as they move seaward. When they are close to the sea, the velocity of their waters is reduced and they drop their loads of solid matter. These particles pile up at the mouth of the river to form the mud flats that become visible when the tides move out.

Salt marshes are formed where the edges of estuaries are sheltered from wave action and the silt and clay particles continue to be deposited as mud. The waters of salt marshes are called the nursery of marine life where prawns, shrimp, and other young crustacea, along with the young of many varieties of fish, are protected from the larger animals that might prey on them. Food is plentiful and the young animals feed and grow until they are ready to move out into the deeper waters.

Sand dunes are interesting in the view they give of the succession of plants on the hills of sand beginning with the grasses that first colonize the bare sand. Dunes are formed on the land and run parallel to the shore line. They are produced by the winds that blow landward carrying particles of sand which drop to the ground and form hills that can reach heights of 100 feet. Grasses first take root and they hold much of the sand together.

Waves sometimes wash away some of the sand facing the sea, but dune-building continues. The plants that manage to take root alter the dune surface, and on their death and later decay, they accelerate the change in the nature of the dune.

The landside of the dune is sometimes moved landward by winds. Over a long period of time, the dunes farthest from the shore are covered by populations of typical land plants. These changes are called succession.

EXPERIMENT 15. Investigating Marine Animals Associated with Seaweeds.

Materials and Equipment. White enamel pan or white margarine tubs; hand lens; field notebook; large plastic jug (gallon size); penknife; ruler or tape measure.

Find a section of the rocky shore with large aggregations of brown seaweeds attached to rocks above the low-tide mark. You will be looking for the variety and numbers of animals for which the large attached algae serve as a minihabitat as well as a source of food for some of them.

The best time to make your observations is from 2 to 4 hours after high tide. Check the tide times for your area with a local newspaper, the weather bureau, an almanac, or local fishermen. When the tide recedes and exposes the large aggregations of seaweeds, they will still be moist.

Fill the plastic container with sea water. Locate an area crowded with seaweeds. Examine one frond down to its attaching holdfast. Look at the bladders filled with air at the free end of the weed. How do the air bladders help the plant? Try to pull the plant away from the rock. Does the holdfast give way or does the plant break first? Use your knife to pry a plant away from the rock. Pour some sea water into the enamel pan and place the seaweed in the water.

Are any small animals in the water that dropped from the plant? Describe what you see. Are any animals still on the plant? Are they moving or feeding? Observe them for a time to get your answer. Make sketches of all the animals you see so you can check them for identification in one of the references in the bibliography (Appendix II). Look closely at the plant surface for any attaching animals that are active. Young barnacles often are found attached to seaweeds. Keep the frond under water and observe the movements of the limbs of the barnacles as they sweep through the water and kick food into the shell toward the mouth opening within.

Are any small snails gliding along the plant surface? If they are, what signs of feeding can you observe? How many snails did you find on a single plant?

A tube-dwelling worm that builds a small coiled tube on seaweeds and sometimes on shells is often found. It is very small and your hand lens will help you see it plainly. It projects delicate gills out of the tube, and finding it will repay you with some interesting observations.

Look also for tiny white or pink very much branched bodies also attached to the surface of the plant. Examine them with your hand lens since they, too, are rather small. They are called hydroids and they are relatives of the corals and jellyfish.

Fill the enamel pan with fresh sea water. Measure a 2×2-foot square of attached seaweeds. Remove all the plants from the square and shake each plant in the pan of water to remove the small unattached animals. They will collect in the pan. They will include small, active crustaceans in some numbers. Check each plant for its attached animals to add to your record of organisms in your field notebook.

Record all the different types you found and an approximate count of each type in your sample. What is the total number of animals associated with the seaweeds in a 4-square-foot area?

EXPERIMENT 16.   Exploring the Microcommunity in a Tide Pool.

This investigation is entirely an observational exercise. The richest tide pools are found in rocky shores. Here, again, it is best to arrive about two hours before low tide. Locate a tide pool and observe closely for all its contained life. There will be attached animals and many free-swimming types. They will include sea anemones, barnacles, hydroids, crabs, small fish, other crustaceans, sponges, and possibly others as well.

What problems of animals attached to rocks near the high-tide marks are not faced by those living in tide pools? Is the tide-pool community a complete community? What is missing? How is the niche that is not part of the community filled? Record all your observations in your field notebook.

EXPERIMENT 17.   Exploring a Sandy Beach.

Materials and Equipment.   Hand lens; field notebook; plastic bags with ties; small hand rake or hand trowel for digging; small pail; a large kitchen sieve, or an 18×18-inch square of plastic screen.

As with every other investigation of seashore life, the variety of plants and animals found varies according to the location. Pacific coast beaches and rocky shores support different types than do similar habitats on the Atlantic. There are good guides to identification for both areas. The important goal is to see living things solving the problems of living in a variety of environments that put them to the test.

The living animals of beaches are more easily found close to the water's edge where the sand is still moist.

Look for small holes in the surface of the sand or for little piles of sand. These are likely to be openings that will lead you to some kind of living thing. Use your hand rake to dig around the holes to a depth of about 3 inches. Deposit the sand on the screening and sift it through. Put the animals you bring to the surface in the enamel pan. Pour sea water into the enamel pan and look for small animals. Sandworms, sand crabs, and sand hoppers are fairly common. Clams, mussels, and small snails are also likely to be found. Record what you collected.

Green and red algae are seen floating in the water at the edge of the beach. On the surface as far as the high-water mark, the tides and waves regularly deposit a new cargo of living things and an assortment of reminders of once-living things.

A large variety of shells is washed ashore. Included may be shells of several types of clams, mussels, scallops, oysters, periwinkles, jingle shells, mud snails, whelks, boat and moon snails, as well as sea stars, sand dollars, sea urchins, and horseshoe crabs.

Occasionally jellyfish, sponges, crabs, sea walnuts, and other living things are brought up on the beach out of the reach of the water for a while, and they die since their bodies, more than 90 per cent water, cannot long survive. In some areas hermit crabs scurry around, with their temporary shell houses, as do fiddler crabs.

Examine any oyster shells you collect and look for small holes bored through the hard shell. These are made either by the boring sponge or the oyster drill—a small snail which thus gets to the living oyster inside the shell and feeds on it.

Among the more interesting objects brought ashore by the tide are the egg cases of the whelk and the skate, a relative of the shark. The skate egg case is a leathery, black, hard, rectangular structure also known as the "Mermaid's Purse." Many of these cases have long, slender projections from each of the four corners. It contains a single egg with a large yolk and surrounding fluid that develops into a living skate.

Whelk egg cases are light-colored, necklacelike, leathery structures, containing many hundreds of whelk eggs—each of which gives rise to a tiny whelk with shells about the size of a pinhead at first. Shake the egg case over a sheet of paper and examine the miniature shells with your hand lens.

The moon snails lay their eggs in the sand in the form of a wide collar they form from sand grains and a sticky substance that holds the grains together along with the eggs. These are often encountered. Sometimes you might even see the snail producing the collar.

Finally there are the shore birds whose activities at low tide are fascinating to watch. They are important consumers of the beach community. Terns, gulls, and sandpipers are skilled, ingenious consumers and scavengers of the beach.

EXPERIMENT 18.   Investigation of Zonation in Rocky Shores.

Rocky shores with steep, almost vertical, walls are usually divided into three distinct zones. These zones are formed by differences in the environmental conditions that exist in each. The types of plants and animals found in each are also different since the ability to live in each zone requires different adaptations.

This investigation requires observation of tide and wave action and the consequences of each on the three zones. After seeing the effects of the water's actions on the environment, look for the kinds of plants and animals each zone supports.

What are the characteristics of the uppermost zone? How does it receive water? How does this represent a problem for its plants and animals? What kinds of plants and animals do you find in this zone? Record your observations in your field notebook.

The middle zone is the largest of the three. How often is it and its living things covered with water? What problems does it present to its plants and animals? What kinds of plants and animals does it support?

The lowest of the three zones is nearly always covered with water. How do its living things differ from those found in the middle zone? What are the main types of organisms found in this zone?

How are the plants and animals of all zones adapted to meet the problems of their environment? How do the animals get their food? How are they protected against water loss? Against the battering force of waves?

EXPERIMENT 19.   Investigation of Variation in One Species of Shell.

Materials and Equipment.   Field notebook; small ruler marked in millimeters; a collection of from 30 to 50 shells of the scallop, clam, periwinkle, whelk, oyster, or any other shell available in quantity.

Variation is a fact of life. No two living things of the same type are exactly alike. They differ in qualities we can measure, and in many others we cannot because we cannot see them.

The shells you collected will differ in color, size, markings, and other qualities. Other types of shell will have characteristic markings, shell thickness, length, and width. Choose a measurable trait or one that can be counted.

Measure each shell in millimeters to the nearest millimeter. What is the range in measurement? That is, what is the difference between the largest and the smallest? How would you determine the average size of the shells?

Arrange the shells in the order of their size. Are there more shells of one length than the others? How can you account for the differences in size? How can you explain the limits of size between which all shells are found?

If you are able to collect scallop shells, you will find that the number of ribs on the outer surface of the shell varies. Count the number of ribs in each shell and then arrange the shells with the same number of ribs in piles. Arrange the piles of shells with the smallest number of ribs at one end and the largest number at the other end, with the intermediate numbers in between. Is there anything unusual about the arrangement?

EXPERIMENT 20.   Investigation of the Plants of Beach and Dune.

Materials and Equipment.   Hand lens; penknife; field notebook; plastic bags and ties.

Beaches and dunes are not the most hospitable environment for land plants. They have little available water and there is a residue of salt that most plants cannot tolerate. Rain percolates through the sand rather rapidly, and the plants are exposed to winds and sea breezes. Water and the dangers of losing water are problems for any plants growing in sandy soils.

Some plants do very well in sand. Many are found along the beaches and on the dunes behind them. These plants seem to flourish and they also serve the habitat by preventing the loss of sand by winds. How are these plants equipped (adapted) to survive?

Among these plants are beach grass (marram grass), beach goldenrod, sea rocket, seaside spurge, beach pea, beach sandwort, bayberry, beach pinweed, false heather, bearberry, jointweed, and saltwort. As you observe the plants of dune and beach, these names will help you to match them with illustrations of plants in reference books. Before long, as you see them again and again, you will associate the name with a specific plant.

Note the structure of the leaves and stems of the plants you find. How are the leaves adapted to reduce the loss of water? Look for hairs on the leaf surface, spines, thick leathery outer surfaces, or thick fleshy leaves. Look also for curled leaves which reduce the surface exposed to the air and very tiny leaves which also reduce the total surface. Examine leaves and stems with your hand lens. Record your observations in your field notebook.

Use a hand rake or hand trowel to dig up the rooted portions of the plants. Shake the roots gently to remove excess sand. Do any have horizontal, underground portions of the stem? If you have removed the plant from the soil with care, you will see that the underground stem may send more than one plant above the surface. How extensive is the root branching? How is this valuable to the plant?

As you move away from the shore and past several dunes, you will begin to find woody plants such as the pitch pine and scrub oak. There may be other varieties of woody plants, depending on the location of the dunes. Are you surprised at their size? What factors might contribute to this result? Remember that the sand dune is a kind of desert. How?

EXPERIMENT 21.   Study of Living Barnacles.

Materials and Equipment.   One-quart widemouthed jars; deep dishes or bowls (can be plastic); plastic gallon jugs; penknife; hand lens.

Barnacles can be collected on small pieces of rock or wood to which they are attached. If you cannot find smaller bits of material with barnacles, use your penknife to separate a small section from a well-eroded larger rock. You can take the barnacles home and maintain them for a few days, if you have enough sea water and you keep them cool and away from direct sunlight.

The barnacle is an amazing animal. It begins life as a free-swimming, immature larvae. As it feeds and grows, it undergoes some changes in appearance. Finally it settles down and attaches itself to some solid object such as wood, stone, or the hull of a boat below the water line.

The attaching cement is one of the strongest adhesives known. Once they are attached to a boat they are very tough to remove. Try to pry one away from its attachment to a rock at the shore.

Collect a few dozen live barnacles attached to small bits of wood or stone. Put them in the widemouthed jar with a supply of sea water. Fill a gallon jug with clear sea water to use at home. Set up a deep dish with some barnacles and cover them with sea water. Observe the animals for their actions. You will see a number of curved, feathery, plumelike, graceful limbs project into the water. The limbs will trap food particles and then sweep them back into the shell opening. Use your hand lens for an enlarged view of the process. When you return home you can set up the container in an appropriate place and continue to observe this interesting animal. Change the sea water daily. Look up the life story of this remarkably well-equipped marine animal in one of the references listed.

A small fraction of the total amount of water on the earth makes up the fresh-water habitats that support an interesting and easy-to-reach group of communities. These range from small streams and brooks to the much wider, deeper, and longer rivers; and from ponds of a variety of sizes to the much larger and deeper lakes; as well as the combination of land and water in marshes and swamps.

All of these habitats have in common the presence of fresh water. Fresh water differs from the salt water of oceans, seas, and bays in a number of ways. Fresh water has very small amounts of dissolved mineral salts. This produces a number of differences in the physical properties of the water. Many bodies of fresh water in colder climates freeze over. Fresh water also weighs less than the same amount of salt water, and thus exerts less buoyant force on bodies in it.

The plants and animals found in fresh-water habitats are unique. They differ from those found in marine waters. But there are the expected producers, consumers, scavengers, and decomposers that are found in any ecosystem. The types of living things that perform the jobs in fresh water are not the same as those in other habitats.

Ponds. A pond is a body of fresh water shallow enough across

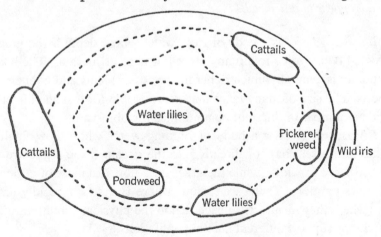

Figure 23. A map of a pond with the areas in which some prominent plants were growing. The dotted lines connect the areas of the pond having the same depth. The depth of the middle of the pond is five feet.

its entire width for rooting plants to grow (Figure 23). In the winter some ponds will freeze completely. During some dry seasons many ponds will dry up. Even in these extreme situations much, if not most, of the pond's living organisms will survive. Ponds are found almost everywhere and the ones you can get to are sure to be a source of endless explorations and investigations (Figure 24).

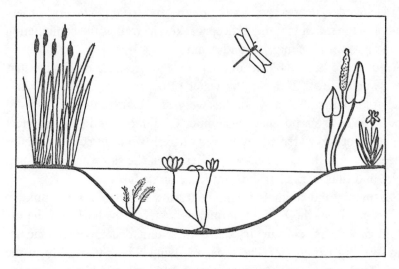

Figure 24.   A sketch of the pond mapped in Figure 23. Why do the areas showing other groups of cattails and water lilies not appear in this sketch?

Lakes.   A lake is a body of fresh water whose depth is too great for rooted plants to be found any place but near its margins. The lake community is generally much richer in species of plants and animals it supports. The size of many lakes makes it possible for a single lake to provide a number of different communities for observation.

Rivers.   A river is a body of running water whose flow finally empties into a sea, bay, or directly into the ocean. Some rivers are a mile and more in width, while the great ones flow distances of a thousand miles or more. There are regions where rivers flow rapidly and others where they meander. In each region the physical conditions differ and they support different animal populations.

If you trace a river back toward its source, it is less and less wide and is more and more shallow. Close to its source the river becomes a stream, a narrow, fairly shallow, rapidly moving body of fresh water.

Streams support communities with relatively few types of plants and animals.

Marshes. A marsh is a wetland, that is, a combination of water and land in which the dominant plants are reeds, sedges, grasses, and cattails. Marsh communities are rich in life and they are equally rich in opportunities to study and investigate them.

In a long period of time, marshes tend to become drier. Woody plants replace the reeds and some of the smaller plants. At this point the wooded wetland is called a *swamp.* Ultimately the area is changed to a forest and it loses its wetland characteristics. Other types of woody plants move in and give the area the appearance of a true forest.

EXPERIMENT 22.   A Study of the Insects in a Pond.

Materials and Equipment.   Peanut butter jars and covers; hand lens; field notebook; kitchen-sieve net with long handle; gallon-size wide-mouthed jar; white enamel pan or margarine tub; gallon plastic jug.

Collect as many aquatic insects with your strainer net as you can from a number of sites around a pond. Make a number of seinings wherever there are pond plants. Pick up some bottom mud with the sieve and pour water through it to wash away the mud and reveal the insects.

Check each collection in the enamel pan half-full of water. Fill your plastic jug with clear water. Add all the insects you collect to the big plastic jug.

When you have a good-sized collection of a variety of insects including water beetles, diving beetles, backswimmers, water boatmen, dragonfly, damsel fly, and May fly nymphs, water scorpions, and others, take them home to examine and study them in depth.

In addition to observations of insects in carrying on their life activities, look for the insects that spend their entire lives in water and those which spend only a part of their lives in water before changing into land-based insects. You may not find the distinction easy to make, but when you check out the specific insects you have collected in the reference works available to you, the life history will make the separation for you.

Set up a fresh-water aquarium in a widemouthed gallon jar. (See Experiment 4, chapter 3.) Add a few aquatic plants and then the collection of insects. You are ready to begin observing.

Look for evidences of feeding. Which insect is the prey (the eaten) and which is the predator (the eater)? Observe any behavior or activity and record it. Some of the insects have gills or other special structures for getting oxygen from the water. What kind of structure is effective in absorbing a large amount of oxygen? Some beetles and other insects come to the surface often and collect a bubble of air which surrounds the body and which glistens like a silvery coat. Look for this kind of respiratory behavior.

Which of your animals are adults and which are in the immature stages? Record any other observations including breeding behavior if you are able to see it or recognize it.

EXPERIMENT 23. The Living Community of a Small Brook or Stream.

Materials and Equipment. Plastic bags and ties; hand lens; field notebook; collecting jars with tight covers; kitchen-strainer net with long handle.

If the stream is a swift-flowing stony brook, collect by hand-picking from stones, logs, and any other drifting materials in the brook. Lift larger stones to look for crayfish which generally lie below the stones waiting for food. The smaller stones will often have smaller insects and small crustacea on them, especially if there are algae attached to the stones. Many small tubes are attached to the stones; sometimes they are built from small bits of plant material or tiny bits of gravel. These are the cases of larvae of caddis flies. Use your hand lens to examine all the smaller organisms you find before putting them in your containers.

Look also for fishes which are likely to be minnows. Use your kitchen-strainer net to collect a few minnows to take home for setting up a small aquarium. The aquarium will enable you to observe the behavior and activities of the minnows in great detail. Collect some small animals from the stream to use as food for the minnows. What larger plants do you find growing at the edge of the stream?

What problems are faced by animals and plants that live in a fast-moving stream? How is each of the organisms you observed adapted to meet the problems? Record all your observations.

How would you go about setting up an aquarium to keep for some time the animals and plants you collected?

EXPERIMENT 24.   Observing the Life on the Shore of a Lake.

Materials and Equipment.   Kitchen-strainer net with long handle; hand lens; field notebook; white enamel pan or margarine tub.

Make a rough-sketch map of the lake shore you will explore. The object is to get a broad look at one part of the lake community.

Collect with your sieve from a number of sites along the shore. Examine the collection in the enamel pan. Make separate collections of animals found in and around the plants; in the sandy or muddy bottoms; and in the surface waters. Record your findings.

What plants did you find along the shore that are rooted in the lake bottom? What plants are floating on the surface and are not rooted? Are there any floating plants that are rooted? Are any plants completely under the water?

Are there any masses of algae floating in the water? Did you see any turtles, fish, frogs, or salamanders? Could you identify them? Record all observations.

EXPERIMENT 25.   Exploration of a Pond, Marsh, or Swamp for Frog, Toad, or Salamander Egg Masses.

Materials and Equipment.   Plastic bags and ties; kitchen-strainer net with long handle; field notebook.

The months of March, April, May, and June are the best for collecting frog, toad, or salamander eggs. The masses of eggs can be seen near the shore with a small part of the mass visible at the surface. Do not take more than a few eggs; leave most of them where you find them. Examine with your hand lens. Has development started? How can you tell?

Fill a few plastic bags with clear water to take home. Set the eggs in a jar with pond water and keep in a cool place out of the direct sun. Keep them until they emerge from the jelly surrounding the eggs. They are now tadpoles. Examine a tadpole for its detailed structure. Are there any limbs? Can you see the gills? What is their function in the tadpole? After you have observed the tadpoles take them back where you found them and release them. The tadpoles will do much better in their regular habitat.

Return to the pond from time to time to collect tadpoles and look for the emergence of legs and the loss of the tail as the water animal, the tadpole, is transformed into the land-living, air-breathing frog or toad.

6 | Investigating Life in Uncommon Places

Living things survive wherever they find the conditions they need. Some types live deep in caves while a few manage to survive at the edge of hot springs. Many living things live in or on the bodies of other living things, often at the expense of the unwilling host. The plant or animal invader is called a *parasite,* and there are very few living things that do not serve as hosts for many parasites. Parasite-host relationships are important factors in ecological situations.

Another unusual relationship is one in which the two living things in the relationship benefit one another. This is the relationship of a simple green plant or alga with a fungus as occurs in lichens. Another such arrangment, as you may recall, is one between a termite and the many one-celled animals (protozoa) that live in the termite's intestine. This relationship is called *symbiosis,* which means living together. Each contributes to the success of the partnership.

There are other less common habitats in which smaller communities of living things do well. Obviously the living things in unusual places are adapted to the special demands made on them by the environment. A number of investigations of less common relationships are described below. They will give you additional ecological insights or they might reveal new relationships; at least, new to you.

EXPERIMENT 26. A Study of Desert Plants and Their Distribution.

Materials and Equipment. Field notebook; tape measure; hand trowel; 4 small wooden stakes; sheets of 8×10 graph paper with ¼-inch ruling.

The desert is a demanding environment. Yet an especially surprising variety of plants has flourished there, and in turn these plants support a variety of animals well adapted to the desert's conditions. If you live close to a desert area, choose a time following the heavy rainfall when the desert blooms in a riot of color and the small herbaceous plants rush through their active but short life spans as they drink in the limited supply of water.

Observe the numbers of brilliantly colored blossoms and the location of the plants in relation to the large, longer-lived desert plants. These are the ones that live for years and their distribution is both interesting and instructive.

Mark off a square area 40 paces by 40 paces. Put small wooden stakes in the corners of the square. Determine the number of different varieties of large plants: cactuses and large woody plants. Use symbols P_1, P_2, P_3, etc., for the different types and record their position on the graph paper.

Measure the distance between 20 pairs of adjacent plants. Select the pairs from different parts of the area being investigated. Record the measurements. Is there any relation between the size of plants and the distance to the next one?

How would you explain the considerable distances between any two plants? What enables the small herbaceous plants to flourish? What causes them to die?

How are the larger desert plants adapted to conserve water? Dig a few small plants from the ground and try to get most of the root out. What does the structure of the root tell you? What is your hypothesis about the roots of the larger desert plants? Why are there so few plants in the open spaces between the larger plants?

EXPERIMENT 27. Observing the Insectivorous Plants in an Acid Bog.

Materials and Equipment. Hand lens; field notebook; boots; hydrion pH paper; a guide to flowering plants (see Appendix II); medicine dropper; sheet of wax paper.

Acid or peat (sphagnum moss) bogs are found in many parts of the United States. They should be visited with caution since the ground in acid bogs is not dependable and it is possible to get into trouble, especially if you are alone. Always visit places such as this with several friends. It is just as rewarding to limit your movements to the edge of the bog.

Check the illustrations of the pitcher plant and sundews in an illustrated guide to flowering plants. These are the most common of the insect-eating plants which are limited to such habitats. The sundews are small and it requires close looking to find them. Pitcher plants are larger and distinctive in appearance. Observe the structure of the sundew and the sticky glands which trap and hold their insect prey with the hand lens. Use your hand lens to observe the inner surface of the pitcher plant. How is this adapted to hold insects in the pitcher?

Measure the pH of water squeezed from some bog plants or from the soil. Use a small strip of hydrion paper and record your measurement. Are you surprised at how acid the bog is?

The most common plant of many acid bogs is sphagnum or peat moss. It makes up much of the surface of a bog. Pick up a handful of sphagnum and allow the water to drip down from it. Now squeeze all the water from the plant. How much water were you able to squeeze out? What happens to the color of the plant? Are there any other distinctive plants in the bog?

Blueberries and cranberries grow in bogs and in the adjoining areas. What would you expect the pH of the soil to be in drier soil where blueberries and cranberries grow? Test the soil to confirm your prediction.

EXPERIMENT 28.   Investigating a Fallen-Log Community—a Microhabitat.

Materials and Equipment.   Hand lens; field notebook; penknife; plastic bag plus ties; tweezers; small jars with screw caps.

Rotting logs in various stages of disintegration are common in all kinds of wooded areas. You can investigate a single rich log over a long period of time or a number of logs in different stages of breakdown which will give you the same general story in a shorter time.

Whatever the method of proceeding, you will want to explore the log community thoroughly and systematically. Begin with the outer surface of the log and look for signs that some animals have burrowed into or out of the log. What are these signs?

The bark may have fungi, such as small mushrooms, bracket fungi, or puffballs living on it. There will also be mosses and lichens on the log surface. These plants do not use the log as a source of food; the fungi do. Lift a section of the bark away from the center of the log.

Use your knife and be prepared to pick up insects and larvae, pill bugs, and other small animals to be put in glass jars for later study. There might be millipedes, centipedes, slugs, ants, wood-boring beetles and their larvae, termites, and many more in the log. Also, you may find the masses of white or yellow threads of the feeding portion of the fungi which along with the bacteria do most of the job of decomposing the log.

Observe and record all the organisms seen in the log. Use your hand lens to check details of structure—especially mouth parts. Can you recognize any of the carnivores (meat eaters)? Plant eaters? Do you recognize any scavengers in the log? What producer supports the array of living things in the log? An oak log needs from 8 to 10 years for complete breakdown by the log community. How long has the log you are observing been disintegrating? Look at the undersurface of the log by gently turning it over. Is there any evidence of soil building from the breakdown of the log? What is it?

EXPERIMENT 29.   Observing the Beginning of Soil Formation.

Materials and Equipment.   Hand lens; field notebook; knife.

The land areas of the earth once had no soil cover. The exposed rocky materials were being broken down by winds, rains, ice, and water. When the first land plants moved onto the land, they were small and were adapted to hold onto rock surfaces. The weathering actions of the physical forces along with chemical influences of the early plants continued the breakdown of the rocks. Plants died and their bodies added something to the soil in the making that gave it some of the properties we look for now. After a long period of time, all these forces produced soil pretty much like the soils of today. Soil building is still going on in many places, and some aspects of the process can be observed.

Mosses and lichens are pioneer plants. They are adapted to living on rock surfaces and they contribute to the disintegration of the rocks as part of soil building over long periods of time. You can find exposed rocks or boulders in wooded areas and adjacent places. Many will already have begun to break down and will have lichens and mosses attached as well as some other plants which managed to find a place in a tiny crevice or in an accumulation of materials in a depression or cavity on the surface of the rock.

Locate a rock invaded by pioneer plants and observe with the hand lens the plants growing on it. Use your knife to pry some plants from the rock. What is the effect of the plants on the rock? What factors other than the plants contribute to the breakdown of the rocks?

EXPERIMENT 30.   Observation of Plants in Some Unlikely Places.

Materials and Equipment.   Hand lens; field notebook; knife.

Man has covered large areas on the earth's surface with asphalt, macadam, and concrete roadways, sidewalks, parking lots, buildings, and other structures. It is remarkable that tiny breaks, crevices, and edges serve as adequate places for some plants to take root. There seems to be enough soil, or opening, for the roots to establish themselves and the plants thrive.

You can observe many instances of plants managing to grow in inhospitable environments by taking a walk near your home. Look for plants growing through asphalt, in parking lots, and at curbside. Use your knife to pry out a number of plants, including their roots. Examine the roots and other plant structures with your hand lens. Record the variety of plants you find.

Are any woody plants able to establish themselves in such sites? What would happen to a parking lot if it was no longer used and was not maintained? Why?

EXPERIMENT 31.   Small Marine Life in Rock Crevices.

Materials and Equipment.   Pooter; hand lens; field notebook; small jars or vials with screw cap covers.

Small crevices in hard or soft rocks making up the rocky shores of ocean and sea are often colonized by a variety of small animals. When light reaches the crevices regularly, the small amount of water trapped in them will also contain some microscopic plants. A crevice is a protected microhabitat. Wave action and tides replace the waters that evaporate and they do not injure or dislodge the life within.

Some attaching forms, such as barnacles, are present, as are snail-like periwinkles and small whelks. Other smaller animals swim freely in the contained water. These can be collected from the water with a pooter as insects are picked up from plants on land.

Record all the types collected and observed. Examine them with the hand lens for details of structure and activity. Snail-like animals will crawl on the inner surface of jars and the method of moving can be observed. You can also see the slitlike mouth opening and the tough, raspy structure for feeding. These animals graze on seaweeds and the marks on the weed show the effects of the tongue. Observe as many activities of the inhabitants as you can.

EXPERIMENT 32. Pitfall Traps for Collecting Small Animals from the Forest Floor.

Materials and Equipment. Pitfall traps; cover traps; hand lens; field notebook.

Sink a one-pound jam or peanut butter jar in the ground of a wooded area so that the top of the jar is level with the top of the soil. Firm the soil around the jar mouth. Pour an inch of water into the jar.

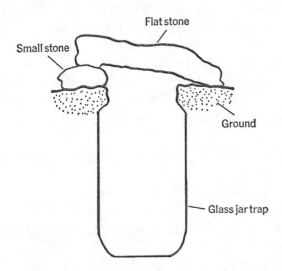

Figure 25. A pitfall trap for collecting forest-floor animals. Baiting with meat or other food will attract other small animals.

Cover the opening with a flat stone supported on one side by a small stone (Figure 25).

A second trap should be set up in another similar site. Bait this one with a small piece of meat. Examine each trap each day for three days. Note the kinds of animals collected each day. After each jar has stood for three days, empty the collections into two clean jars for inspection, identification, and note taking. Are the animals attracted to the bait different than those that fell into the water-filled trap? Use your hand lens for closer inspection of each animal. Are any winged animals present? Are any types more numerous than the others? How many different types did you catch with each trap?

Another type of trap easy to set up is a cover trap. Water a section of bare ground in a wooded area and cover with a large flat stone or a piece of flat board. Examine after a day and record the results. How do the cover-trapped animals compare with those caught in a pitfall trap?

OTHER SUGGESTED EXPERIMENTS AND INVESTIGATIONS.

1.   Make a complete collection of plant galls in a wooded area. Allow as many as you can to complete the development, in closed containers, of the gall insect within.

2.   Investigate the edge of a swamp or marsh for signs of succession, that is, notice that woody plants are beginning to establish themselves and the land is becoming drier.

3.   Make a study of spiders and the webs they build. Also observe webs of different spiders for the types of insects they trap with their webs.

4.   Investigate the habitats that support populations of mosses and lichens.

5.   Observe the feeding behavior of shore birds such as gulls, terns, and sandpipers.

6.   Study the development of fresh-water snails. The egg masses will be encountered frequently in pond collections.

7.   Investigate the animals in forest leaf litter collected with a Berlese funnel (Figure 26).

8.   Keep regular records of small animals observed in and under logs and boards in woods through the winter.

9.   Study the fleshy fungi (mushrooms) of the forest floor.

10.   Investigate the bracket fungi in an oak-hickory forest.

11.   Collect and germinate tree seeds from trees such as maples, ashes, hickories, and others.

12.   Study the feeding habits of marine snails.

13.   Investigate insect-plant relationships in a field or meadow.

14.   Study the activities and life cycle of slugs.

15.   Investigate fiddler and other crabs in an estuary.

16.   Study the stages of decomposition of a log until soil is the final product.

17.   Study the frogs and toads of your area.

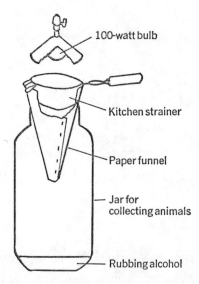

100-watt bulb

Kitchen strainer

Paper funnel

Jar for collecting animals

Rubbing alcohol

Figure 26. A Berlese funnel for collecting the animals of leaf litter. The heat of the 100-watt bulb drives the animals from the litter through the strainer into the jar.

18.   Rear adult insects from larval stages in rearing cages.

19.   Investigate the behavior of the water flea, Daphnia.

20.   Investigate the relation of temperature to luminescence of the firefly.

21.   Make a study of the shrub layer of a maple-beech forest.

22.   Keep a calendar of the flowering date of spring flowers and major tree flowers in an oak-hickory forest.

23.   Make a collection of the delicate marine red algae and mount and dry it on white cards.

24.   Study hermit crabs and the types of shells they use.

25.   Observation of one species of trees, e.g., a sugar maple, a shag bark hickory, a white oak, or a tulip tree, through a year of its life. Keep records of flowering time, time leaves emerge, time fruit and seeds are ripe, and the time when insects and other pests appear.

26.   Collect butterfly or moth caterpillars and feed them in rearing cages until pupae or cocoons are produced. Keep the cocoons in a cage with a small amount of moisture until adult moths or butterflies emerge.

27.   Observe the flowers of woodlands that blossom and flourish before the leaves of the trees above them emerge.

7 | Investigating Living Things Indoors

When you are young, the time you can give to exploring and investigating the world of life is limited. Your schoolwork and preparation must come first. Then there are the chores around the house as well as the other things you are interested in. When you get the chance to wander through a forest, along a rocky shore, or around a small pond, you see much more than you can immediately resolve. Questions and ideas run rapidly through your mind as you begin to notice the things around you. What enables a plant to thrive where it does and why did you not see it in another place? What kind of food does a dragonfly eat? How does the golden orb spider construct so beautiful a web which looks just like all other golden orb webs? You are stimulated to want to know.

Many of the questions that puzzle you can be studied by bringing living things into your home. There you can set them up in appropriate minienvironments and can give them the environmental conditions to get some of the answers you seek. You can make observations whenever you have the opportunity. Often you can observe events you would not be able to see in the natural environment. If you set up a small pond and stock it with animals and plants you want to observe as they perform their life supporting activities, your small aquarium is a window that allows you to look into the interior of the pond.

Many of the smaller animals have life histories that last days, weeks, or sometimes months at the most. By establishing them in appropriate containers you can observe them frequently. In this way you will be able to fill in details of the life histories of some of the organisms.

You can also investigate the behavior of some of the smaller organisms.

Do not bring into your home any living things you do not intend to study, and be sure you set them up under conditions they require. Be particularly careful not to overcrowd any minienvironment. It is better to have a smaller number of organisms than too many. Above all, give the attention and care needed to maintain your community as long as you want to observe it. Add water when needed, remove the animals that die, and discard the minihabitat when it has served its function for you.

Aquaria and terraria in which you establish water and land communities require a variety of containers which you can improvise. Gallon-size widemouthed glass jars; two-pound-size widemouthed glass containers; all glass or metal-frame commercial aquaria (2- or 5-gallon size); clear plastic containers of all sizes; small peanut butter jars; small plastic or glass vials with caps; cardboard or wooden boxes which can be used as breeding or rearing cages by providing them with windows of plastic, glass, or screening; milk cartons for seed germination and for growing small plants; metal containers of a variety of sizes, from which you can build apparatus to your special needs, are all likely materials for this type of recycling use.

EXPERIMENTS AND INVESTIGATIONS.

EXPERIMENT 33. Setting Up and Observing a Terrarium with a Rotting-Log Community.

Use as large a glass container as you have available. A five-gallon aquarium would be ideal. By bringing in a small section of a log with its contained life, you can use a smaller container.

Collect a section of a rotting log with its contained community. Put it into a large plastic refuse bag. Secure the opening tightly. Collect enough forest soil with a trowel to cover the bottom of your terrarium with a layer about one inch thick. Carry the soil in a smaller plastic bag.

If the log contains termites, it is a good idea to try another log. It is not wise to bring termites into the home. They might escape by accident, or as a result of carelessness, and their potential for damage to the house is too great to risk. Most other log animals are not likely to be a problem.

Place the soil in the terrarium and distribute it over the bottom. Place the log in the terrarium in the position it was in when collected. Add enough water to keep the habitat moist. Cover the top of the aquarium with a glass or plastic plate, or its own cover if a large jar is being used. Keep the terrarium in a cool place and away from direct sunlight.

Observe whenever you can. Many living things are to be found in any log undergoing disintegration. Its surface probably has fungi, lichens, and mosses. There may also be spore cases of slime molds attached to the bark of the log. Inside there may be slugs, centipedes, millipedes, ants, spiders, beetles, insect larvae of a number of types, as well as eggs of a number of kinds of small animals. Look for signs that some animals move between the log and the soil. Record all organisms you observe and any behavior that looks noteworthy.

EXPERIMENT 34. Setting Up and Observing a Terrarium with a Forest-Floor Community.

Use the same kind of container as for the rotting-log community. Collect some stones from a wooded area along with enough forest soil to form a two-inch layer above a layer of gravel or a mixture of gravel and sand. Carry your collections in plastic bags. A few larger flat stones will make an attractive addition to the terrarium.

Use a hand trowel to collect small sections of earth covered with moss plants, a small fern or two with the soil it is growing in, a few tree seedlings, and some creeping ground plants, such as wintergreen or partridgeberry, with their roots intact. Put each plant in a separate plastic bag for transportation. If you find a small frog, toad, or salamander, take them with you for the terrarium.

Set up the terrarium by putting a thin layer of gravel and sand on the bottom. Cover with the forest soil, and plant the individual plants in the soil. Place the mosses and the stones in appropriate places and add the animals. Moisten the terrarium and cover with a glass plate, a plastic cover, or a piece of fine screening. You might try sinking a small, oval plastic cup in the soil to serve as a pond.

Keep the terrarium in a cool place away from direct sunlight. Add water to keep the proper level of moisture. Observe when you can. Add other small animals if the community is not crowded. Record all observations you think worth noting.

EXPERIMENT 35.   Setting Up and Observing a Desert Community.

The same kind of container can also be used to set up a desert terrarium. Use clean, washed sand as a surface. Do not make the surface level. Create the impression of small hills by piling up sand in a few places. Add a few small stones using a larger one to form an overhang. Local florist shops and many variety stores sell small cactuses which can be planted in the sand. One or two fleshy leaved, small succulent plants would make a good addition to the plants of the community.

Animals can be purchased from local pet shops or tropical-fish shops. The gentlest of the desert animals to use is the horned lizard. If you are able to get an animal, be sure you have a dependable supply of ants, pill bugs, or similar non-flying insects. If you cannot obtain an animal, the plants alone make an interesting and attractive minienvironment that shows only the desert producers. Do not water the plants too often. Add water to the sand near each plant about once every three weeks. Do not overwater.

EXPERIMENT 36.   Set Up and Observe a Pond Aquarium.

You had an opportunity to set up and observe a pond ecosystem in Experiment 4. The objective then was to identify the different niches in a pond ecosystem and to identify some specific animals and plants that filled some of the niches.

The pond ecosystem in a gallon-size widemouthed jar or in a 2- or 5-gallon aquarium can be set up as described in chapter 3. It can be maintained for a long time to observe and study the behavior, life histories, adaptations, and other activities of specific organisms. How are they equipped to get food, to move, to get oxygen, and other adaptations? Are their eggs laid in water and do they give their eggs any special care?

You can add small pond fish as the main predator animals, to observe feeding and other behavior. Tadpoles can be added, when available, to observe the transformation into frogs. Pond snails can be studied for locomotion, egg laying, development, and feeding.

EXPERIMENT 37.   Set Up and Observe a Small Marine Aquarium.

Use a gallon-size widemouthed jar to set up a short-term marine environment. Collect a gallon or more of sea water and filter it through a coffee filter to remove the larger particles. Put about one inch of clean beach sand in the aquarium to serve as the bottom.

Collect some floating green seaweeds such as the sea lettuce or others to serve as the producers of your aquarium. Collect a few small hermit crabs, a small starfish or sand dollar, some live small snails, and a few barnacles attached to a small stone to serve as consumers.

After the aquarium is established, collect some marine plankton with your plankton net. The tiny microscopic plants and animals will provide food for the barnacles, especially. A few other marine organisms might do well for a week or more; animals such as a small sea urchin, a small fish, a green crab, or others as available. Some aquarium supply shops now feature marine animals for such aquaria and if available and not too expensive you might get some that you want to observe in great detail.

Observe regularly and note special features of feeding behavior, movement, and other behavior. If there are signs that the aquarium is not doing well, dismantle it. If kept in a cool shaded place, it should provide you with some interesting observations.

EXPERIMENT 38.   Using Breeding and Rearing Cages to Observe Stages in the Development of a Variety of Insects.

Breeding and rearing cages can be made from a wide variety of boxes and plastic containers (Figures 27 and 28). To make breeding cages you will need an assortment of cardboard boxes, sheets of plastic, plastic tape, sheets of screening, plastic covers, plates, or dishes to cover screen cages, aluminum foil.

If you make breeding cages from cardboard boxes, use at least half of one side for the window. Cut the window opening out cleanly and add a window of clear plastic attached with plastic tape. Make a small box tray to fit the bottom of the cage of aluminum foil. You can then add a small container with water to provide moisture needed by the insects without wetting the box.

To make a screen cage, cut a rectangular piece of screening 30 cm.×20 cm. Form a cylinder with the screening with a small overlap. Tape the overlap firmly with plastic tape. The diameter of the cylinder will be about 3½ inches while its height will be about 8 inches. Use a plastic cover from a margarine tub, an ice cream, or similar container, to serve as the bottom of the cage. Put a small amount of clay around the inside of the cover. Push the screen cylinder into the clay so the screen has a firm support. Use a similar cover to serve as

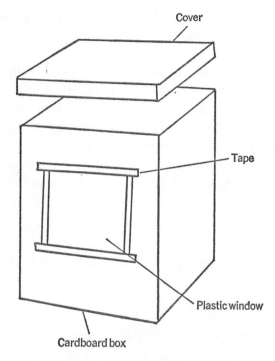

Figure 27. A cardboard-box breeding cage with a plastic window for observing developing small animals.

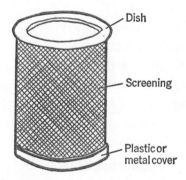

Figure 28. An insect breeding cage made of plastic or metal screening.

the top, or use a small dish or similar object. Each should have a large transparent plastic window or one made of screening.

When larvae of a number of insect types such as butterflies, moths, and beetles are collected, it is necessary to provide them with food.

Caterpillars are usually collected on the plants they use as food. Collect a supply of the leaves of the food plant to keep the animals supplied with food.

Rearing cages can also be used to observe stages in the life histories of a large number of small animals. Land snails, slugs, pill bugs, and many other such animals. Slugs and snails will feed on lettuce leaves, while pill bugs will flourish if a slice of raw apple or raw potato is added to the cage and changed every few days.

Moth cocoons, butterfly pupae, praying mantis egg cases, and similar structures of other insects can be observed until the adults or young nymphs emerge.

EXPERIMENT 39.   To Determine the Relation Between the Frequency of Flashes of a Firefly and Temperature.

Collect a number of fireflies and keep them until used. Put a single firefly in a small vial closed with a screw cap. Use a watch with a second hand to time the frequency of flashes which can best be observed in dim light.

Measure the number of flashes in 15 seconds at room temperature. Immerse the vial containing the firefly in a container of warm water for two minutes. Count the number of flashes in 15 seconds.

Immerse the vial in ice water for two minutes and count the number of flashes in 15 seconds.

What is the relation between temperature and frequency of flashes in the firefly? Repeat the procedure with five new fireflies. How do the results compare with the first trial? What would the result be if the temperature was closer to boiling water than the one you used and lower than the temperature of ice water? Try both and determine whether your original conclusion was valid. How would you determine the optimum (best) temperature for fireflies?

EXPERIMENT 40.   To Determine the Viability of Seeds of Wild Plants.

The viability of seeds is their ability to germinate and produce new plants. Every seed produced by a plant does not give rise to a new plant. But the successful varieties of plants are those that produce enough new offspring to maintain the type. Viability is expressed as a percentage figure. If 100 seeds are planted and 95 of them germinate, the seeds are 95 per cent viable.

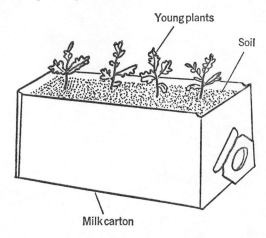

Figure 29. A milk-carton planter for germinating seeds and growing young plants.

Milk cartons make excellent planters in which viability studies can be made (Figure 29). They can also be used to start plants from seeds or from cuttings. The young plants can then be set out in natural areas in environments favorable to their survival.

In planting seeds in milk-carton growers, use soil from the habitat in which seeds are collected. Collect the seeds of a dozen common herbaceous plants, as well as the seeds of some trees and shrubs. Keep each type of seed in a different labeled envelope.

Plant one to two dozen seeds in each grower. Keep in a shaded place and water enough to keep the soil damp—not wet. Count the number of plants that emerge. Calculate the viability and express it as a percentage. If you planted fewer than 100 seeds of any one type, is your viability dependable? What is the advantage to a plant of the ability to produce thousands of seeds?

Appendix I

LIST OF EXPERIMENTS
BY CHAPTERS

CHAPTER 2

EXPERIMENT   1. To Measure Some Properties of Soils.

          A. pH of the Soil.

          B. Water-holding Capacity of the Soil.

          C. Soil Structure

EXPERIMENT   2. To Measure Some Properties of Pond Water.

          A. pH of Pond Water, Aquarium Water, and Swamp Water

          B. Temperature of Fresh Waters.

          C. Light Penetration in Water.

CHAPTER 3

EXPERIMENT   3. To Observe and Study the Structure of a Pond Community.

EXPERIMENT   4. Setting Up and Observing a Minipond Ecosystem.

EXPERIMENT   5. An Introduction to a Woods' Ecosystem (Spring, Summer, and Fall).

EXPERIMENT   6. Exploring a Meadow, a Field, or a Vacant Lot (Spring Through Fall).

CHAPTER 4

EXPERIMENT   7. Observation and Study of an Abandoned Yard.

EXPERIMENT   8. A Study of Some Food Chains in a Schoolyard.

EXPERIMENT   9. To Observe the Colonization of a Small Section of Bare Soil.

CHAPTER 7

Appendix II

A LIST OF BOOKS TO WHICH YOU CAN REFER FOR HELP

The books included in this list were very carefully selected. Many are likely to be found in small local libraries. Most of the books include large numbers of excellent illustrations which can be used in identifying the things you find. The illustrations total in the thousands. Most of the books are paperbacks and are sold in variety, department, and other stores. This is particularly true of the 14 books in the Golden Nature Guide Series of Golden Press.

A. Books in Ecology

Buchsbaum, R., and Buchsbaum, M., *Basic Ecology*. Boxwood Press, 1959.

Farb, Peter, *Ecology*. Time-Life Books, 1963.

Hungerford, H. R., *Ecology: The Circle of Life*. Childrens Press, 1971.

Pringle, L., *Ecology: Science of Survival*. Macmillan, 1971.

Storer, J. H., *The Web of Life*. Devin-Adair, 1956.

B. Books to Use for Their Wealth of Illustrations in the Identification of Living Things You Find. They Also Include Details on Behavior, Life Histories, and Where They Are Found.

Alexander, T., Burnett, R. W., and Zim, H. S., *Botany*. Golden Press, 1970.

Barrett, J., and Yonge, C. M., *Collins Pocket Guide to the Sea Shore*. Collins, 1967.

Buchsbaum, R., *Animals Without Backbones*. Univ. of Chicago, 1947.

Buchsbaum, R., and Milne, L. J., *The Lower Animals. Living Invertebrates of the World*. Doubleday, 1960.

Cochran, D. M., *Living Amphibians of the World.* Doubleday, 1961.

Fichter, G. S., and Zim, H. S., *Insect Pests.* Golden Press, 1966.

Gilliard, E. T., *Living Birds of the World.* Doubleday, 1958.

Herald, E. S., *Living Fishes of the World.* Doubleday, 1961.

Klots, A. B., and Klots, E. B., *Living Insects of the World.* Doubleday, 1959.

Levi, H. W., Levi, L. R., and Zim, H. S., *A Guide to the Spiders.* Golden Press, 1968.

Lyneborg, L., *Field and Meadow Life.* Blandford Press, 1968.

Mandahl-Barth, G., *Woodland Life.* Blandford Press, 1966.

Palmer, E. L., *Fieldbook of Natural History.* McGraw-Hill, 1949.

Peterson, R. T., *A Field Guide to the Birds.* Houghton Mifflin, 1947.

Peterson, R. T., *A Field Guide to Western Birds.* Houghton Mifflin, 1960.

Peterson, R. T., *A Field Guide to Wildflowers of North Eastern and North Central North America.* Houghton Mifflin, 1968.

Petrides, G. A., *A Field Guide to Trees and Shrubs,* 1958.

Reed, C. A., *The Bird Guide.* Doubleday, 1948.

Sanderson, I. T., *Living Mammals of the World.* Doubleday, 1955.

Schmidt, K. P., and Inger, R. F., *Living Reptiles of the World.* Doubleday, 1957.

Shuttleworth, F. S., and Zim, H. S., *Non-Flowering Plants.* Golden Press, 1967.

Swain, R. B., *The Insect Guide.* Doubleday, 1948.

Wherry, E. T., *Wild Flower Guide.* Doubleday, 1948.

Zim, H. S., and Gabrielson, I. N., *Birds.* Golden Press, 1956.

Zim, H. S., and Shoemaker, H. H., *Fishes.* Golden Press, 1956.

Zim, H. S., and Martin, A. C., *Flowers.* Golden Press, 1950.

Zim, H. S., and Cottam, C., *Insects.* Golden Press, 1956.

Zim, H. S., and Hoffmeister, D. F., *Mammals.* Golden Press, 1955.

Zim, H. S., and Smith, H. N., *Reptiles and Amphibians.* Golden Press, 1953.

Zim, H. S., and Martin, A. C., *Trees.* Golden Press, 1956.

Zim, H. S., Fisher, H. I., and Burnett, R. W., *Zoology.* Golden Press, 1958.

C. Books on the Ecology of a Wide Variety of Habitats, Large and Small. You Can Refer to These Books for Details of the Structure of the Habitat and Its Physical Properties and the Structure of the Communities That Live in the Different Habitats. These Books Are All Magnificently Illustrated.

Amos, W. H., *The Life of the Pond*. McGraw-Hill, 1967.

Amos, W. H., *The Life of the Seashore*. McGraw-Hill, 1966.

Berrill, N. J., *The Life of the Ocean*. McGraw-Hill, 1966.

Hoffman, Melita, *A Trip to the Pond*. Doubleday, 1966.

Klein, S., *A World in a Tree*. Doubleday, 1968.

Klots, E. B., *The New Field Book of Freshwater Life*. G. P. Putnam, 1966.

Neal, E. G., *Woodland Ecology*. Harvard, 1963.

Niering, W. A., *The Life of the Marsh*. McGraw-Hill, 1968.

Reid, G. K., Zim, H. S., and Fichter, G. S., *Pond Life*. Golden Press, 1967.

Ricketts, E. F., and Calvin, Jack, *Between Pacific Tides*, 4th ed., revised by J. W. Hedgpeth. Stanford Univ. Press, 1968.

Schwartz, G. I., *Life in a Drop of Water*. Natural History Press, 1970.

Schwartz, G. I., and Schwartz, B. S., *Life in a Log*. Natural History Press, 1972.

Southward, A. J., *Life on the Seashore*. Harvard Univ. Press, 1965.

Sutton, Ann, and Sutton, Myron, *The Life of the Desert*. McGraw-Hill, 1966.

Thorson, Gunnar, *Life in the Sea*. McGraw-Hill, 1971.

Yonge, C. M., *The Sea Shore*. Atheneum, 1963.

Zim, H. S., and Ingle, L., *Seashores*. Golden Press, 1955.

D.   Some Books Containing Suggestions for More Experiments in Ecology.

Brown, V., *How to Explore the Secret Worlds of Nature*. Little, Brown, 1962.

Klein, R. M., and Klein, D. T., *Discovering Plants*. Natural History Press, 1968.

Polgreen, J., and Polgreen, C., *Backyard Safari*. Doubleday, 1971.

Pringle, L., ed., *Discovering Nature Indoors*. Natural History Press, 1970.

Pringle, L., ed., *Discovering Nature Outdoors*. Natural History Press, 1969.

Appendix III

SOURCES OF SUPPLY

The major source of supply for many of the materials you need in making equipment and devices for your investigations is your own home. Bottles, jars, plastic containers, plastic bags, aluminum foil, kitchen utensils that are no longer needed, wire coat hangers, scraps of wood, Saran Wrap, vials, and other containers, as well as rubber and plastic tubing, corks, nails and screws, nylon or cotton fishing line, and a thousand and one other things. Storekeepers in your neighborhood might be willing to save boxes, trays, and other materials for you that they would otherwise discard.

In the event that these sources are not able to provide all you need, look to restaurants and school cafeterias for gallon-size, widemouthed glass jars in which they get pickles and mayonnaise. These must be washed thoroughly before you can use them.

For kitchen utensils and almost everything else you need in constructing apparatus, look to hardware, housewares, and variety stores as well as the department stores which often feature such materials. Beyond these sources, the companies listed below carry a wide range of materials used in ecological work. A number of them are supply houses that provide all such materials to science teachers for their use in teaching. All have catalogues, but some are huge, expensive volumes and they might be unwilling to send one to an amateur naturalist. Some suppliers have abridged catalogues for which you can send. The term catalogue or abridged catalogue will appear after each one willing to send them to you. To be sure, send a post card of inquiry first.

Aquarium Stock Co., 31 Warren Street, New York, New York 10007. For marine aquaria and animals. Catalogue.

Carolina Biological Supply Co., Burlington, North Carolina 27215 and Gladstone, Oregon 97027. For hydrion paper, living animals, hand lenses, aquarium, and terrarium supplies. Abridged Catalogue.

Central Scientific Co., 1700 W. Irving Park Road, Chicago, Illinois 60613. For the same materials as are available at Carolina Biological. Abridged Catalogue.

Edmund Scientific Co., 605 Edscorp Bldg., Barrington, New Jersey 08007. Hand lenses, pH papers, and many other supplies. Catalogue.

General Biological Supply Co., 8200 S. Hoyne Avenue, Chicago, Illinois 60620. Same range of supplies as Carolina and Central. Abridged Catalogue.

Gulf Specimen Co., P. O. Box 206, Panacea, Florida 32346. For marine animals. Catalogue.

Herbach and Rademan, 41 E. Erie Avenue, Philadelphia, Pennsylvania 19134. For plexiglas sheets of assorted sizes, in thicknesses running from $\frac{1}{16}$th of an inch to $\frac{1}{4}$ of an inch, as well as other plastics. Catalogue.

Wards Natural Science Estab., P. O. Box 1749, Monterey, California 93940, and P. O. Box 1712, Rochester, New York 14603. Hand lenses, aquarium and terrarium supplies, pH paper, and live animals.

Any lumber and building supplies company can be approached for scrap wood, dowel sticks to use as handles, and plastic sheets as well as screening.

Index

ABOUT THE AUTHORS

GEORGE I. SCHWARTZ AND BERNICE S. SCHWARTZ are coauthors of *Life in a Log*, which was awarded Honorable Mention by the New York Academy of Sciences for excellence in the field of science books for young readers.

BERNICE S. SCHWARTZ, coauthor of *Food Chains and Ecosystems*, has moved her interests from beachcombing in the Rockaways of New York City to forested areas wherever they are to be found. It is really a continuation of her lifelong interest in the many worlds of living things. GEORGE I. SCHWARTZ, following a long career in teaching, hopes to continue his writing, along with his wife, who will also contribute to the illustrating of their books. Princeton, New Jersey, is their present home and is the point from which their frequent trips to wood and shore originate. Mr. Schwartz is the author of *Life in a Drop of Water*.

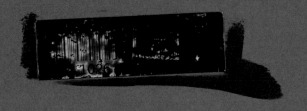